**A TRAINING COURSE IN
HOW TO LEAD SMALL GROUPS**
INCLUDES TRAINEE SESSIONS

GROWTH GROUPS

COLIN MARSHALL

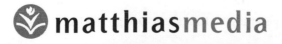

Growth Groups
© Matthias Media 1995

Matthias Media
(St Matthias Press Ltd. ACN 067 558 365)
PO Box 225
Kingsford NSW 2032
Australia
Telephone: (02) 9663 1478; international: +61-2-9663-1478
Facsimile: (02) 9663 3265; international: +61-2-9663-3265
Email: info@matthiasmedia.com.au
Internet: www.matthiasmedia.com.au

Matthias Media (USA)
Telephone: 724 964 8152; international: +1-724-964-8152
Facsimile: 724 964 8166; international: +1-724-964-8166
Email: sales@matthiasmedia.com
Internet: www.matthiasmedia.com

ISBN 978 1 875245 40 6

Cover design and typesetting by Lankshear Design Pty Ltd.

CONTENTS

CONTENTS CONTINUED

INTRODUCTION

This course is all about how to lead a Growth Group. A Growth Group is a place where Christians can grow. It is also a catalyst for the growth of the gospel. If you want to lead fellow believers toward Christian maturity and together reach others for Christ, this training is for you.

In today's church there is a proliferation of small group ministries. It is a new barometer of success in church growth. Pastors are quizzed about how many small groups they have operating and what percentage of members are in them. Larger churches have full-time staff members coordinating the small group program.

All kinds of groups are running: friendship groups, discussion groups, prayer groups, special interest groups, mission groups, Bible study groups, evangelism groups, support groups, koinonia groups, covenant groups. Small groups are being promoted as the key to revitalizing the church. They are seen as the way to transform nominal adherents into active participants— dying churches into growing concerns.

In many ways, the church has just jumped onto the small groups band-wagon. Secular researchers have developed theories about groups—why they work and the methods to use in them. This has been applied in most spheres of human enterprise: business, government, education, health and so on. Small groups with trained leaders have significant impact on individuals and organizations.

There is every reason for Christians to gain from this new area of social research and harness the power of small groups. In the general community, people are being transformed through small groups. Addictions are overcome; deep emotions are dealt with; skills are developed; personalities are moulded; the overweight are trimmed down. These groups are potent environments and Christians ought to be attracted to any strategy which changes people for the good.

But we need to answer some basic questions to ensure our small groups are an expression of gospel ministry and not just 'christianized' versions of humanistic techniques. Questions such as:

- What is gospel ministry?
- What are the distinctive elements of a Christian small group?
- What growth does God desire in people?
- How does God bring about his transformation of people?

In this course, we grapple with these questions as well as learning the skills of leadership. In the end, we will see that there is such a thing as a distinctive Christian group. We call it a Growth Group.

WHO WILL USE THIS COURSE?

Growth Groups is for any Christian or group of Christians committed to equipping leaders of God's people. It is designed to train leaders who can teach the Bible and pray with other Christians. It will prepare leaders to gather together fellow-believers in evangelistic enterprise. In short, it will equip leaders to grow Christians and grow the gospel. The course is for anyone who wants to pursue these ends.

WHAT IS IN THIS COURSE?

Despite appearances, this is not another book about small group ministry. *Growth Groups* is:

- A 10-week practical 'hands-on' training program to develop effective Growth Group leaders.
- A training program useful for all Christian ministry, not just Growth Groups, because it deals with the fundamentals of gospel work.
- A central idea—that as small groups flourish in our society generally, we are faced with the need to define what is distinctive about **Christian ministry** in small groups.

The *Growth Groups* training course consists of:
- 15 training topics (following this introduction)
- 10 training session outlines for trainees (found in the back of this *Growth Groups* manual)
- 10 training session outlines for trainers (sold separately as *Growth Groups Trainer Notes*)
- appendices.

If you are doing this course as a **trainee**, you will need your own copy of this *Growth Groups* manual.

If you are doing this course as a **trainer**, you will also need to buy the *Growth Groups Trainer Notes*.

HOW TO USE GROWTH GROUPS

Growth Groups is designed to be used in a training group. A trainer gathers together a small group of Christians into such a group. The trainer needs to have had some experience of ministry in small groups, but doesn't have to be a world expert! The *Trainer Notes* provide plenty of tips for trainers, and the session outlines are easy to follow.

It would be best to limit the number of group members to around 10, to ensure everyone has opportunities to practise their skills. Your group could be as small as two people. The group meets for 10 one-hour sessions. An hour is the minimum time needed to get through each session. If you can meet for longer, the training will be more effective.

During the session, the group will engage in a number of different activities. As well as prayer and some Bible discussion, the training group will undertake three types of activities. These activities are represented by 'icons' on the training session outlines.

 PRACTICE: In a practice exercise, group members practise leading a Bible discussion. Usually, a couple of group members will be asked to observe the rest of the group as one member leads the others in a practice Bible discussion. The group then analyses how the discussion went.

 MIRROR: The mirror exercise gets the group to reflect upon how it has been operating, in order to learn something about small group dynamics. These exercises require the group to discuss how they went about an activity they have just completed.

 TOPIC: The topic exercises involve the trainer leading the group in a discussion of the training topics set for that session. Sometimes questions are provided for the group to answer; sometimes the discussion will be more free-form. It is unlikely that there will be time to read through the relevant training topics for each session, so trainees must have read them **before** the group meets. Not every training topic is directly addressed in the training sessions. However, it is expected that trainees will read all of the topics over the duration of the course. They may bring to the group discussion questions or comments about these extra topics.

WHAT ARE THE GOALS OF THE COURSE?

The goals of the *Growth Groups* training course are two-pronged. There are **broad goals** which explain why it is worthwhile to train leaders to run small groups for Christians. These aim to impart the philosophy of small group ministry upon which this course has been built. And there are **specific goals** for the trainees concerning the skills and understanding they will need to acquire in order to be Growth Groups leaders. Both sets of goals are outlined below.

Broad goals of training

1. To equip leaders with the vision, attitudes, knowledge and skills to initiate and lead a Growth Group.
2. To train leaders as Bible teachers/pastors rather than small group facilitators.
3. To develop an understanding of small group ministry shaped by the Bible.
4. To impart a vision for the ministry of Growth Groups, teaching trainees to think through a long term, expansive strategy of how Growth Groups can contribute to winning the world for Christ.

Specific goals for trainees

At the end of the course, trainees should be able to:

1. Identify good and bad habits of interpreting the Bible
2. Prepare a Bible study
3. Lead a Bible study
4. Analyse what makes a discussion succeed or fail
5. Assist in a Bible study
6. Lead a prayer time
7. Get started in one-to-one ministry
8. Diagnose the symptoms of an unhealthy group
9. Start a Growth Group

The strategy of growth groups

Christians meet in many kinds of groups for a variety of purposes: church committees, property maintenance, choir, youth groups, ministry training, sharing and support groups. Some of these are task-oriented groups; some are for friendship; some are for teaching and input. Groups such as these tend to have a primary purpose, as well as secondary consequences, such as building closer relationships between the group members.

This diversity of groups and purposes is valid. However, there is such a thing as a distinctively Christian group with a distinctively Christian purpose. This type of group is the subject of this training course. We could quite properly call it the Christian group. Instead, in this course we call it a 'Growth Group'.

1.1 MINISTRY GOALS FROM COLOSSIANS

What are the goals of a Growth Group—its primary purpose, the reason for its existence? What is the ministry of a Christian group? To answer these questions, we need to consider the reasons Christians meet and the instructions given to groups of Christians in the New Testament. By doing this, we discover God's word and his agenda for Christian groups, which usually are called churches.[1]

Throughout our training we will study Colossians, so let's begin by formulating some goals for Growth Groups from this epistle. We could use any New Testament letter to the early churches or, more properly, study them all, since all are God's word to us. For practical reasons we will look at Colossians, asking this question: What are the essential aims for a Growth Group?

Possibly the topic sentence of Colossians is 2:6-7:

> So then, just as you received Christ Jesus as Lord, continue to live in him, rooted and built up in him, strengthened in the faith as you were taught, and overflowing with thankfulness.

"Receiving" Christ in these verses is not referring to some sort of mystical encounter where Christ enters our hearts. It has to do with something that the Colossians were 'taught' (in v. 7). We don't usually think of 'receiving' a teaching or a piece of information, but that is the word that the New Testament often uses to describe the way that the gospel was passed on from person to person, and generation to generation (cf. 1 Cor 15:1ff). When the Colossians 'learned' the gospel (from Epaphras, 1:7), they received Christ.

Here, in chapter 2, the apostle is appealing to them to remain steadfast in their faith in this gospel, in the face of legalistic alternative gospels, and to continue to accept Christ's lordship over daily living.

We take our goals for Growth Groups from this instruction. We define our goals as:

- TO RECEIVE CHRIST AS LORD
- TO LIVE WITH CHRIST AS LORD

The goals of Growth Groups are Christ-centred, not group-centred. Let's look in some detail at what it means to receive Christ as Lord and to live with his Lordship.

---

1   One of the issues worth pondering during this course is the distinction between 'church' and 'small groups'. There may be logistical and structural differences between them, but are there any *theological* differences?

Receive Christ as Lord

When the Colossians received the gospel of Christ, and put their trust in it, they received Christ Jesus himself. They were once slaves in the dominion of darkness (1:13), but now they are "in Christ" (see 2:6, 7, 10, 11, etc.); now they have all the fullness of God that was in the Son. We cannot drive a wedge between Christ and the gospel of Christ—as if we become Christians through hearing the gospel but then get to know Christ personally later on. We only know Christ as he comes to us in the gospel, offering us redemption and reconciliation with God. This is why Paul can describe his whole ministry as proclaiming Christ: "We proclaim him, admonishing and teaching everyone with all wisdom, so that we may present everyone perfect in Christ" (Col 1:28).

Thus, imparting right knowledge and understanding is central to Christian groups. Receiving Christ means being taught something; it is about learning and understanding and wisdom and knowledge. Salvation and godly living depend on these things, and they are only to be found in Christ. In our groups, we therefore aim to:

- understand God's grace in all its truth (1:6)
- be filled with the knowledge of his will through all spiritual wisdom and understanding (1:9)
- have the full riches of complete understanding, in order that we may know the mystery of God, namely, Christ, in whom are hidden all the treasures of wisdom and knowledge (2:2-3).

The Scriptures teach us many things about Christ. As we learn these things, take them to heart, and put our trust in them, we grow in our personal knowledge of Christ. He reveals himself as he speaks through the Bible, and we get to know him as a person, as we learn and embrace **all that he is**, and **all that he has done for us.**

All that he is (1:13-20, 2:9-10):

- the image of God
- the creator
- the owner of creation

- the reason for creation
- before creation
- the sustainer of creation
- the head of his church
- the beginning
- the firstborn from among the dead
- the fullness of God
- supreme
- the head over every power and authority

All that he has done for us:

Throughout Colossians, the main verbs describing God's saving work suggest the richness of his grace in Christ:

- qualified   to share in the the inheritance of the saints (1:12)
- have   redemption, the forgiveness of sins in the Son (1:14, 2:13)
- rescued   from the dominion of darkness (1:13)
- transferred   into the kingdom of the Son (1:13)
- presented   holy in his sight, without blemish and free from accusation (1:22)
- made full   in Christ (2:10)
- circumcised   in Christ, putting off the sinful nature (2:11)
- buried   with Christ in baptism (2:11)
- made alive   with Christ (2:13)
- died   with Christ to the basic principles of the world (2:20)
- raised   with Christ through faith in the power of God who raised Jesus (2:12)
                 with Christ (3:1)
- will appear   with him in glory (3:4)

In knowing Christ, we are rescued from the dominion of darkness and brought into his kingdom of light. This is what faith is—it is personally knowing Christ; it is understanding who he is and what he has done for us in such a way that we put all our trust and reliance in him.

But now he has reconciled you by Christ's physical body through death to present you holy in his sight, without blemish and free from accusation—if you continue in your faith, established and firm, not moved from the hope held out in the gospel.

COLOSSIANS 1:22-23

Receiving Christ is never an academic or merely intellectual exercise. It is a relationship of personal knowledge; it is a relationship of trust based on what we have learnt. Our Growth Groups must stimulate people to receive Christ in this way, and to continue strong and steadfast in the face of many alternatives.

Live with Christ as Lord

The knowledge of Christ as Lord and Saviour entails living with Christ as Lord. This means:

Remaining faithful—rejecting other lords and their religions

In the salvation of Christ we are full and complete, needing no supplementary religious knowledge or duty. Our faith must be in Christ alone.

See to it that no one takes you captive through hollow and deceptive philosophy, which depends on human tradition and the basic principles of this world rather than on Christ. For in Christ all the fullness of the Deity lives in bodily form, and you have been given fullness in Christ, who is the head over every power and authority.

COLOSSIANS 2:8-10

The prohibitions on religion are repeated throughout: we ought not be deceived by fine sounding arguments (2:4); we are not judged by what we eat and drink (2:16); we ought to avoid false humility and the worship of angels (2:18); we must not be puffed up, lest we lose connection with the Head (2:19).

In contrast, we are twice exhorted to continue: continue in our faith, established and firm, not moved from the hope held out in the gospel (1:22-23); and continue to live in him (2:6). Epaphras' prayer is also our group prayer: "that you may stand firm in all the will of God, mature and fully assured" (4:12).

Submitting to Christ in every sphere of life

"And whatever you do, whether in word or deed, do it all in the name of the Lord Jesus, giving thanks to God the Father through him" (3:17). The source of this new life is not immediately apparent to the world, for it is a life "now hidden with Christ in God". Christ is our life, but this will only be revealed when Christ appears (3:3-4).

Other verbs in Colossians highlight the totally transformed life of the Christian:

- live   a life worthy of the Lord (1:10)
- please   the Lord in every way (1:10)
- bearing fruit in every good work (1:10)
- strengthened with all power according to his glorious might (1:11) in the faith (2:7)
- have   endurance and patience (1:11)
- giving thanks to the Father, joyfully (1:12) to God the Father through Christ (3:17)
- be thankful (3:15)
- overflowing with thankfulness (2:7)
- set   your hearts on things above (3:1) your minds on things above, not on earthly things (3:2)
- put to death whatever belongs to your earthly nature (3:5)
- rid yourself of all such things as these (3:8)
- put on   the new self, which is being renewed in knowledge in the image of its Creator (3:10) love (3:14)
- clothe   yourselves with compassion, kindness, humility, gentleness and patience (3:12)
- bear with   each other (3:13)
- forgive   as the Lord forgave you (3:13)
- let   the word of Christ dwell in you (3:16)
- submit   to your husbands (3:18)
- love   your wives (3:19)
- obey   your parents (3:20)
- do not   embitter your children (3:21)
- obey   your earthly masters (3:22)

- provide   your slaves with what is right and fair (4:1)
- devote   yourselves to prayer being watchful and thankful (4:2)
- be wise   in the way you act toward outsiders (4:5)

The sum of the Christian life is continuing to live in:
- faith   in Christ Jesus (1:4, 2:5)
- love   for all the saints (1:4)
- hope   in what is stored up for us in heaven (1:5)

1.2 GROWTH GOALS

An image used repeatedly in Colossians is *growth*. This provides us with another way of expressing the purpose of Growth Groups—and a way of explaining their name.

Gospel growth

Paul rejoices in the growth and fruitfulness of the gospel (1:6). His commission is to proclaim Christ to everyone, including the Gentiles (1:24-29) and he can say that the gospel "has been proclaimed to every creature under heaven" (1:23). He calls for prayer for his world-wide mission and exhorts the Colossians to be wise in winning outsiders (4:2-6).

Christian groups are committed to the spread of the gospel. They are created by hearing the word of truth (1:5), so they naturally share in the gospel enterprise.[2] To evaluate our Growth Groups we should ask: Is the gospel reaching more people through our group?

Christian growth

The gospel grows and bears fruit by transforming people. We are to grow in the knowledge of God (1:10) and it is God who causes the body to grow, through connection with Christ the Head (2:19). Epaphras prays for growth towards maturity (4:12).

---

2   More on this in training topic 9: *Gospel growth through Growth Groups*.

Our goals for Christian growth can now be summarized:

- **to receive Christ as Lord**, which means personally knowing and trusting Christ:

  all that he is, and

  all that he has done.

- **to live with Christ as Lord**, which means:

  remaining faithful—rejecting other lords and their religions, and submitting to Christ in every sphere of life.

To evaluate our Growth Groups, we should ask:

- Are our group members receiving Christ as Lord?
- Are they living with Christ as Lord?

Growth group basics

2.1 THE ACTIVITIES OF GROWTH GROUPS

There are limitless possible activities and programs for small groups: eating, singing, therapy, sports, reading books, problem sharing—almost any activity involving personal interaction.

But what are the activities *basic* to Growth Groups?

Prayer

Calling upon the Father through his Son is the way we begin and sustain the life of faith. It is the natural disposition of children towards their father. It is the cry of utter dependence on God for salvation and growth.

In Colossians, we see Paul thanking God and praying for the growth of the church (1:3-14), extolling the prayerfulness of Epaphras (4:12) and calling on Christians to pray for the proclamation of Christ (4:2-6).

In Growth Groups, we pray for ourselves and others in group prayer and as prayer partners.

Learning God's word

We can only respond to God in the prayer of faith if we know his will. Prayer to a silent deity is foolish superstition. But we are not in that position, because God has spoken. He has spoken in his Son, whom we know through the written word of the Spirit. God has revealed his will for his people, for their salvation and godly living.

The Colossians have heard the word of truth, the gospel (1:5), and Paul asks God to fill them with a knowledge of his will so that they may live a life worthy of the Lord and please him (1:9-10). He then sets out the word of truth about God's Son and the completeness of salvation in him (1:15-2:23), and the kind of life that is worthy of the Lord and pleasing to him (3:1-4:18).

In Growth Groups, we learn God's word through Christ-centred Bible study and we encourage each other to obey it.

Proclaiming God's word

Those who have received God's mercy in his Son want all the world to know. Christianity is contagious. It spreads through Christians telling others the good news of God's grace in Christ.

Paul points out that the gospel is growing around the world (1:6). Epaphras brought the word of Christ to the Colossians (1:7); Paul is now teaching this same word (1:27-29) and the church is to pray and work for Christ to be preached throughout the world (4:2-6).

Through Growth Groups, we proclaim Christ to others, both personally and through various group activities.

2.2 THE ADVANTAGES OF GROWTH GROUPS

Having discussed the basics of Growth Groups, you might be asking yourself: don't all our Christian meetings and structures have the same goals and activities?

The answer is 'yes'. Whether they be large groups at church, conferences, Sunday schools or whatever, all Christian gatherings should be geared towards gospel growth. So, why have Growth Groups? What is the distinctive contribution of Growth Groups in gospel growth?

Growth Groups have advantages in many ways.

Learning the Bible

There are several advantages to learning the Bible in a small group context.

Large groups also sport some of these advantages, but they are particularly enhanced in a small group.

Learning how to read the Bible

In a talk or sermon, the speaker does not have much time to explain the process of interpreting a particular passage. Sometimes he or she can do this, but often he just has to give the bottom line. In a discussion group, more time can be devoted to establishing good methods of interpretation. False methods of Bible reading, such as ignoring contexts or 'spiritualizing' Old Testament passages, can be courteously and individually corrected in the small group.

Applying the Bible

In a sermon, the whole congregation can be challenged to make application in certain areas. In a small group, however, each member can think through personal applications in more detail. Struggles in applying the Bible can be shared and there is time for prayer for each other. Small groups can provide a sense of accountability where members help each other act upon decisions to change.

Educational factors

Small groups aid the education process by:

- engaging people's minds more effectively than in a larger group
- providing the opportunity to verbalize ideas, thereby promoting understanding and unveiling confusion or error
- enthusing group members to read the Bible, because of the process of self-discovery in the group discussions of passages[1]
- allowing members to ask questions to clarify the material being taught
- providing the opportunity to explore further ideas of interest or relevance
- allowing the leader to ask questions for understanding and application, thus getting immediate feedback
- tailoring the content and method of teaching to the group members.

---

1   We must be careful not to elevate self-discovery to being a Christian virtue. The goal is to hear God's word, whether from the preacher, the group discussion or from private reading. However, the understanding we come to through mental effort and group discussion often has the greatest impact on us.

Prayer

A small group allows for prayer which is more personal and comprehensive. Individuals can share more personal information for prayer; more matters of prayer can be covered; there are opportunities to teach the group how to pray. Furthermore, reports of God's response to our prayers can be shared.

Training and using people's gifts to multiply ministry

In larger meetings, there are many opportunities for serving each other, from both the 'platform' and the pew. However, in small groups these opportunities are multiplied and it is often easier to see what needs to be done—bringing supper, contacting an absent member, leading in prayer, leading a discussion, organizing a bush walk. The small group is an ideal context to help every member be a minister.

Small groups are excellent for training members in a variety of skills—leading a prayer time, leading a Bible study, music leading, nurturing new Christians and so on. The small group provides on-the-job experience and a 'safe' environment for learning and making mistakes.

Communication of church vision and plans

A network of small groups within a congregation provides a way of holding the church together with a unified purpose and direction.

The small group leaders need to channel information in two directions. They need to educate and enthuse the group about the vision, goals and programs of the church, as well as collecting feedback from the group members concerning their spiritual health and ideas for the program. Through the leader, they can express their needs and their reactions to church life.

This work of relating the group to the larger church is essential. It is too easy for small groups to become disaffected with church life, develop an independent party spirit and weaken commitment to the wider congregation. This is a particular danger for groups meeting over many years with little variation in membership.

The loyalty of the leader to the wider congregation and its leaders is the key to this unifying function of small groups.

Shepherding

Small groups provide a means of knowing each other more personally. Larger meetings allow for some conversation between individuals, but time is limited and their structure makes this level of interaction difficult. Small groups enhance communication between individuals, providing the opportunity to hear each other's thoughts, ideas, problems and questions. Personal relationships are developed where there is practical, honest concern for each other. The Bible can be applied to the issues of day-to-day life.

Growth Groups are rather like sheep pens, gathering Christians into a context where they can be protected and nurtured by the Bible, pray and support each other. It is difficult to monitor who is at a large meeting, but we know immediately if a small group member is absent. We become aware of those who are struggling, or perhaps dropping out of Christian faith, and bring them back into the pen.

Establishing new members and new Christians

Growth groups are a key to incorporating new Christians and members into the larger fellowship. As they make friends in the smaller group, they will feel less isolated in the large group.

Reaching the world through Growth Groups

Growth Groups provide a strong foundation for evangelism. When Christians meet together in Bible study and prayer, evangelism should be a natural outcome because we discover that at the heart of God is the salvation of the world.

Every new Growth Group is a home base for evangelism as the members work together to reach others. We therefore need to plant Growth Groups around the world in every corner of society.

One of the advantages of Growth Groups is their simplicity. Any Christian with a vision of studying the Bible and praying with other Christians can get started. In towns or cities where there are no Christ-centred churches, we can start a Growth Group with just three or four other like-minded believers.

If each Growth Group spawns a 'daughter group'—a new Growth Group— every couple of years, there will be a multiplying effect, as more Christians grow in Christ and bring the gospel to others. Outgrowing your Growth Group is a great goal to have!

Pitfalls for growth groups

3.1 DANGERS IN SMALL GROUPS MINISTRY

There are some worrying trends in the small group movement within the church. You can detect the dangers in this kind of testimonial from a small group member.

> *We had a great time in our small group last night. I was able to talk about my brother's illness for the first time. There were lots of tears and hugs and we prayed together for healing and faith. We really felt the presence of God. It was a little taste of heaven. Actually, I'm finding the whole small group experience is bringing me closer to Jesus as we get closer to each other. There is a real sense of community, not like at church on Sundays. It's great being able to let others know what is really going on inside and then feel accepted for what we are. And as we experience God's healing in us we can reach out to others in need. There is a real sense of mission together.*

The small group movement has developed its own buzz words, words like 'community', 'experience' and 'mission'. At first glance, these words and ideas seem to be fundamental to Christianity, and we are attracted to the kind of ministry reflected in the testimonial above. However, in small group ministry such words are now loaded with meaning and connotations which need to be challenged. The buzz words expose some of the dangers in Christian small groups—dangers which threaten the heart of the gospel.

Community

God himself is three eternal persons in relationships of love and unity. The Father loves the Son, speaks to the Son and sends the Son into the world. The Son loves the Father, obeys the Father, prays to the Father. The Spirit is sent from the Father and Son to glorify the Son.

God created man and woman for relationship; people are social beings by God's design. Mankind's rebellion towards God and his created order is exposed in the breakdown of relationships we experience in this world. The biblical story of the Fall is the pattern of all human experience— ever-widening circles of evil from deep within the heart of man, posing a permanent threat to the possibility of community.

Onto this scene comes the gospel. The gospel is God's work of reconciliation, a work of restoring the community of God and humanity. This most profound healing power is found in the cross, where the curse of sin is broken. On the cross, the Father forsook the Son, breaking an eternal communion for the sake of the restored communion of God and man.

Christians are thus bound together in a new society of those who belong to Christ, and we are being transformed by him. The distinguishing mark of Christian disciples is love, as we share in genuine community with honesty, unity, forgiveness and good deeds. We wait for heaven, the perfect community where all enemies of loving relationship are crushed under the feet of the risen Lord.

If *relationships* are fundamental to Christianity, what dangers can there be in stressing community in small groups?

- The purpose of the group can easily focus on the development of human relationships. A successful group is seen to be characterized by intimacy, vulnerability, openness, forgiveness and so on. This emphasis on human relationship is often at the expense of knowing God and the salvation of Christ. JI Packer observes that there has been a shift in the purpose of small groups in the last 25 years: "It is not so much thought of as a way of seeking God as much as seeking Christian friends. The vertical axis is not emphasized as much as the horizontal axis."[1]

---

1   Quoted in W Bird, 'The Great Small Group Takeover', *Christianity Today*, 7 February 1994.

It is not that prayer and Bible study are absent, but they are seen as tools to create community.

- The distinctiveness of Christian groups can be lost. The activities are irrelevant because any group following the principles of small group theory will result in intimacy. Look at what happens in Weight Watchers, AA groups, special interest groups and social clubs. They all provide a sense of genuine community. The problem in many Christian small groups is that they are no longer distinctively Christian.

- The formation of community is often not rooted in the gospel of Jesus' death for sinners. Small groups can draw together on a multitude of bases: personal needs, political agenda, stage of life, interests and so on. But groups of Christians are built on one distinct and unique foundation, being children of God through faith in his Son. If the gospel is not at the heart of the group, it may be a group of Christians but it is not a Christian group.

- Groups preoccupied with community tend to become problem-centred. They become highly introverted, focusing on their own needs. If community is the aim, the ideal group is open, accepting and affirming—a haven for broken, alienated lives. It is very attractive, because we all have times of hurt, grief and disappointment living in this sinful world. A group that will put its collective arm around us and give a reassuring hug is not a bad idea. But such a group becomes problem-centred. The energy of the group is directed toward those with problems, and we all have problems all the time!

Christian groups are not primarily about helping people with their problems. You probably can't believe you just read that! It sounds positively *unchristian*. But it is true. The focus of Christian groups is *growth*, not problems. We are seeing this in our study of Colossians.

Take the case of someone in your group who is unemployed. In a problem-centred group, she will feel free to talk about this, the group will listen and empathize. They will ask at appropriate times how the job hunt is going and even join in searching out employment for her. They will be aware of associated problems such as self-esteem, and try to talk this through. When her cash flow gets really tight, they discreetly pass round the hat and buy a week's groceries. Others who have been retrenched in the past become particularly helpful.

What a great group to be in! Who could ask for more? You could. Such a group, although made up of Christian people, is not distinctly Christian. There are many support groups in the community which would do the same things—some better, some worse.

In a growth-centred group, all of this will be done, and more! The distinctly Christian element is to pursue growth in the knowledge of God and obedience to him. So prayers will be offered, not only for a job, but for faith in Christ, patience, endurance, avoidance of self-pity and so on. Through group and private discussion, the unemployed woman will be strengthened in the great truths of God's providence and taught to see her situation through God's eyes. In other words, she will be helped to grow as a Christian.

- If community is the goal, the small group has become the end rather than the means. Instead of meeting to hear and respond to God in his word, the functioning of the group is central. True Christian ministry will see small groups as a means to an end, in the best sense of the phrase. In relationship with each other, we teach the gospel and pray and spur each other on toward godliness of mind and action.

To summarize, our primary reason for joining a Growth Group must not be to get closer to each other, but to grow in Christ.

Experience

The enthusiastic testimony given for small groups above expresses a common sentiment: that the small group experience brings people closer to God. 'Experience' is another groups buzz word, because it is a profound experience to meet regularly in a small group. This is especially true in a society hell-bent on isolation and privacy. But for some who promote the small groups movement in the church, the experience of intimacy in the small group has become everything. They urge that the reality of God is found primarily in the experience of being close to others in a small group and finding 'healing' of emotions and hurts through this closeness. In this way, the group is said to bring us right into the presence of God.

There are several dangers with this view, which severely undermines the gospel.

- We create our own small group god. If we determine God's character and will from the small group experience, we will create our own small group god. This imaginary god may have little resemblance to the one true God. Our small group god might be welcoming and affirming, but is unlikely to be the God who wiped out Pharaoh for his insolence or who killed Ananias and Sapphira for their lie to the Holy Spirit! Such a God would be too discomforting in a small group experience. We will have moved from Christian revelation to mysticism.

- Our faith can be in the small group experience, not in Jesus' mediation. If the small group makes God real to us, and brings us closer to God, our salvation lies in the quality of that group experience. Presumably, in some groups we would be deemed further from God because the experience is diminished. This has moved a long way from the absolute assurance of God's favour for those who cling to the cross of Christ.

- Experience is the god of this age. We can create all kinds of small group experiences, from songs of praise to primal screaming. Who can tell what they mean? Of course we feel great in a warm affirming group, but to label this feeling as being 'closer to God' is an unwarranted leap in thinking.

Mission

Small groups easily become small teams. Significant things can be achieved through a disciplined, committed team with common goals. This leads small group supporters to talk a lot about mission. The mission of the group will be defined by what the group perceives itself to be achieving. If it is aiming for community, it will want to draw others into that community. If it is working for experiences, it will seek to share those experiences with others.

The net effect of these goals can be to see mission in social terms, with evangelism as an optional extra. Mission becomes a 'horizontal' activity—between one another—rather than a 'vertical' activity—bringing others to God. The preaching of the death of Christ to a dying world is too often seen as a narrow understanding of mission, one that is out of touch with a holistic (another buzz word) view of meeting all human needs.[2]

---

2   We will look at this issue further in training topic 9: *Gospel growth through Growth Groups*.

3.2 THE ANTI'S OF SMALL GROUPS

There are some further implications of the small group focus on community, experience and mission. If these are misunderstood, small group ministry can become:

Anti-preaching

The value of proclaiming the word of God is diminished in favour of small group discussion and personal discovery. The experience of the group process in Bible reading is prized above the actual message. The sermon is seen as an inferior context for learning about God, because the experience may be less than scintillating. This is not what we want. Small groups ought to generate a thirst for good preaching, because they develop a hunger for God's word.

Anti-the minister

Small group ministry has become a lay movement, responding to perceived deficiencies in the churches. It can be a way for the laity to take power for themselves, in competition with congregational pastors. Some parts of the small groups movement are avowedly 'anti-clerical'. It is right to see the limitations of only having the professionals do the work of ministry. Small groups are a superb way for every Christian to get involved in ministry. However, this must not be an expression of mutiny, rejecting the authority of recognized, trained, Bible-teaching pastors.

Anti-the church

The closeness of community in small groups is prized above the total congregational life. In short, group members reduce commitment to church. This is a disastrous result and creates isolated, unaccountable groups each doing what is right in their own eyes and not pulling together to make the whole church more fruitful.

Preparing
a Bible study

One of the goals of this course is to provide training in preparing a Bible study from scratch. We hope to show you how to start with a passage from the Bible and design a discussion which will teach that part of God's word.[1]

4.1 UNDERLYING PRINCIPLES IN DESIGNING A BIBLE STUDY

The nature of the Bible: God's word through human authors

The principles we use in interpreting the Bible are derived from our doctrine of Scripture—we believe it is God's word given to us through human authors. Because the Bible is God's word inspired by the Spirit, we must pray for understanding. Our comprehension and response to the Bible is first and foremost a work of God in us. However, because God has used human authors, the actual method of Bible study we use is the same as for any

---

1   Appendix II: *Using pre-packaged Bible studies* addresses a related issue.

comprehension of literature.[2]

As well as communicating the meaning of the Bible, the studies we prepare should teach good habits for interpreting the Bible.

The nature of learning: whole—particulars—whole

In any study process, it is helpful to get an overview of the subject before studying the details. The details will make more sense in the light of the whole and, in the end, the details will shape our understanding of the whole. In more technical terms, if we suggest a thesis, then subject it to analysis, we come up with a synthesis.

We could say that a 'learning loop' is in operation. The following diagram illustrates this concept.

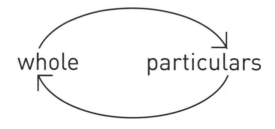

4.2 THE FOUR STEPS

There are four steps in preparing a Bible study:

Step #1	Understanding the passage
Step #2	Applying the passage
Step #3	Working out teaching goals
Step #4	Packaging the study

---

2   There is a lot more that can be said about the important issue of understanding the Bible. See appendix I for suggested reading on this important topic.

Step 1: Understanding the passage

The following are some questions to ask yourself as you endeavour to understand the passage from which your study will be drawn. We don't usually follow strictly the order below when we are looking at a Bible passage, but this approach helps us to analyse the process involved.

Overview of the book

Getting an overview of the Bible book from which our study passage is taken helps us avoid taking parts of the Bible out of their context. God gave us his word in the form of normal human documents. One part of a document needs to be understood in relation to the whole.

When reading through an entire Bible book, ask yourself these kinds of questions:

- What are the main themes?
- What words or phrases are repeated?
- What do I learn about the author and recipients?
- What appears to be the author's purpose in writing this book?

Overview of the passage

Read through your chosen passage several times:

- What stands out?
- What do I find difficult to understand?
- What key words are repeated?
- What ideas are repeated?
- Are there specific commands to be obeyed?
- Are there warnings to heed?
- What did I learn about the writer or recipients?
- Who are the main characters?
- When and where does this take place?
- From my first impressions, what are the main ideas in this passage?

Question bombardment

Interrogate the passage by bombarding it with your questions. Try to unravel your questions and anticipate the difficulties the group might have.

- What ideas are hard to understand?
- What words are unfamiliar?
- Why has the author written in this way?

Background

What background information—history, politics, geography, customs—is important?[3]

- Am I given any historical details in the passage?
- Does the passage seem to refer to customs which we may not understand today?
- Do any of these background details seem essential to understanding the passage?

Flow of the passage

In working out the structure and logic of a passage, we come to see the writer's flow of ideas.

- How does this passage contribute to the overall message and purpose of the book?
- What is its immediate context?
- What is the flow of the passage?
- Does the author use:

  —repeated words or ideas?

  —linking words like *and, but, although, how much more?*

  —explanatory words such as *because, for, so that, therefore, since, if ... then, in order that?*

  —words which indicate time such as *now, after, then, when?*

The passage in biblical context

Ask questions like these to establish the biblical contexts within which your passage can be seen.

---

3   Study resources: Atlases, commentaries, histories and dictionaries can be helpful in unraveling difficulties in the biblical text. However, it is important to work at our own study first, rather than jumping straight into the commentaries. After using a commentary, it usually is hard to think creatively about a passage. We tend to give commentaries more authority than they deserve.

- Is the passage quoted elsewhere in the Bible, or does it quote another Bible passage?
- What major biblical themes are dealt with in this passage?
- Does the passage contain fulfilment of promises or contain promises which are fulfilled later?
- Where does the passage fit into God's saving work in history?
- What does the passage say about who Jesus is and the purpose of his coming?

Central truth and supporting truths

Your chosen passage may make many points and touch upon many truths. However, if we try to teach everything all at once, the study will be indigestible. Fortunately, we often find that a writer focuses on a main idea or subject, and the other topics mentioned are directed to this central truth. It is a valuable exercise to seek to determine this central truth.

- what is the main point of the passage?   central truth
- how does the writer establish this main point?   supporting truths

Step 2: Applying the passage
Avoiding application

The application of a Bible passage concerns how it has impact upon our lives—how it applies to us. We have all seen Bible studies which end up in the theological stratosphere and are not grounded in life and action. It's safer to stay up in the clouds—hitting the ground hurts. And it's often more fun up in the clouds, speculating about angels and pinheads.

A common experience in Bible study groups is to 'tack on' to a study some sort of token application of what has been discussed—because we know we shouldn't leave it out altogether. But we often only come up with superficial comments about how God's word should affect us. These may sound familiar:

- **The after-thought application**. A hurried two minute addendum to the discussion with a question like: "How does this passage apply to us?"
- **The stock-standard application**. We drag up the same guilt-induced applications no matter what passage is at hand. Usually, these involve

our prayer life, Bible reading, evangelism and using our time better.

- **The point-the-finger application**. We can avoid application by saying: "God's not saying much to me here, but I sure wish so-and-so could hear this."

Types of passages

In terms of application, there are two broad types of Bible passages:

- Passages with explicit commands for faith and obedience (e.g. Proverbs, sections of the Gospels, much of the Epistles).
- Passages with no explicit commands, but which reveal God's character and purposes (e.g. Old Testament history, prophecy, sections of the Gospels, Acts). We apply these passages by committing ourselves to God's character and purposes in faith and obedience. This kind of application is more implicit than explicit, as we see below.

Types of applications

- **Belief applications:** Many passages have to do with our beliefs and doctrine. We apply these by correcting our false ideas and confirming what we already know to be true.
- **Behaviour applications:** Some passages have to do with our behaviour, practices and attitudes. We apply these by planning and implementing changes in our lives, wherever appropriate.

We can fall into a trap here by separating behaviour from belief. Christian belief or conviction always results in changed behaviour, practices and attitudes. And Christian behaviour can only be derived from true doctrine. Belief and behaviour go hand-in-hand. The value of distinguishing between them is to ensure that we don't twist the meaning of a Bible passage by improperly applying it.

Variety of applications

In teaching the Bible, we need to be studying in two ways:

- studying the text of the Bible
- studying the context of the group.

To apply the Bible to our group we need to be studying and understanding our group members and the context in which they are living as Christians. They are individuals with their particular issues in obeying God, but the word of God also addresses their broader contexts such as our group, the church and the wider society with its values and beliefs.

So we can apply the passage in four possible directions:

- **The individual:** How does this passage help him or her make progress in understanding the Bible, godliness and ministry to others? What circumstances, beliefs, values and attitudes in his or her life does this passage address? Will the people in my group believe the central truth and supporting truths?[4]

- **The Growth Group:** From this passage what changes should we make to our group activities and relationships to each other?

- **The church:** What doctrine, practices, traditions, priorities or attitudes in our local church are not consistent with this part of God's word?

  What doctrines and practices of the wider church around the world are corrected by this passage? Think about the church and denominational background of your group and discuss any false ideas they may have grown up with. Contrasting these with the Bible will sharpen their grasp of gospel truth.

- **The world:** How does this part of God's word correct the values, beliefs and behaviour of our society? What social, ethical and intellectual trends are at odds with this passage? These applications help us grasp the distinctiveness of Christianity.

Step 3: Working out teaching goals

Our teaching goals can now be derived from Steps #1 and #2. Having clear teaching goals will keep the discussion moving forward toward a conclusion and provide the basis for designing questions in Step #4.

Teaching goals cover both understanding and application.

---

4   Aside: As a leader, you can see how important it is to develop personal relationships with the group through relaxed, unstructured times over meals, supper or outings together. The more you know your flock, the more incisive your teaching will be.

Goal: central truth

Write down the central truth in a clear simple sentence.

At the end of the study, I want the group to understand ...

Goal: supporting truths

You won't have time to discuss every supporting truth, so choose one or two which are most important for understanding the central truth. Write down the supporting truths you want to focus on.

At the end of the study, I want the group to understand ...

Goal: application

Again, you won't be able to discuss every possible application. Choose those which relate to the central truth. Write down one or two changes of belief or behaviour in clear simple sentences choosing the issues most relevant to your group.

At the end of the study, I want the group to make these changes ...

Step 4: Packaging the study

This is the creative part of preparation where you craft questions that will allow the group to unravel the truths and applications of the passage.

Leading a good Bible study is a bit like giving at Christmas time. You carefully wrap up presents and take them to family and friends, who then delight in unwrapping each parcel and discovering the treasures inside. Packaging the study is like wrapping gifts which you take to the group for them to sit around and unwrap. The wrapping is your questions and the gift is God's word. The group delights in finding God's word as the discussion process opens up the Bible's meaning and application.

Designing questions

Work out questions which will draw out the central truth, supporting truths and applications from the passage. Often the questions you wrestled with in your preparation will be useful.

The types of questions you can use include:
- **Observation questions**

  To help the group see the basic content and structure of the passage.

These should be easy to answer.
- **Interpretation questions**
  These are more difficult but more exciting, as they cause the pennies to drop.
- **Correlation questions**
  To show how the passage is related to the rest of the book and the whole Bible.
- **Summary questions**
  To draw the passage together and lead people toward the central truth. They also clarify the structure or flow of the passage.
- **Application questions**
  To think through the concrete belief and behaviour steps that arise from the passage.

The launching question

This is the last step, but the first question—to work out an engaging introduction to the discussion.

A launching question should be:
- Purposeful—introducing the main ideas or applications that will be addressed.
- Interesting—engaging the group's attention and arousing their minds.
- Easy—making them the experts so all can contribute early in the discussion.
- Open—with many possible answers.

There are two general types of launching questions:
- Topical—to raise the issues related to the goals of the study, by posing a dilemma or asking opinions.
- Textual—to raise an issue in the text being studied which will help to unravel the whole passage.

Preparation sheet
COLOSSIANS 1:15-23

STEP 1: UNDERSTANDING THE PASSAGE

Overview of the book

Overview of the passage

Question bombardment

Background

Flow of the passage

The passage in context

Central truth and supporting truths

STEP 2: APPLYING THE PASSAGE

The person

The group

The church

The world

STEP 3: WORKING OUT TEACHING GOALS

Central truth

Supporting truths

Applications

STEP 4: PACKAGING THE STUDY

Observation questions

Interpretation questions

Correlation questions

Summary questions

Application questions

Launching question

Leading a Bible study

The skills required for leading a Bible study are well worth developing. In practical terms, they are like any other skills—once you have learned the basics, the key to improving is to get plenty of experience. If assistant leaders in your group or other friends can give you constructive feedback, you will find it of great benefit.[1]

5.1 PRINCIPLES

There are two basic principles in leading a discussion. At first glance, they appear to be contradictory.

Control: the leader is a teacher, not just a facilitator

In studying the Bible we are dealing with the truth of God's word. We are not just airing opinions; rather, we are seeking to understand God's revelation of himself. Each part of the Bible can be rightly interpreted and our discussion ought to aim to clarify this meaning so we can respond to God's word. There

---

1   Training topic 7: *The games people play* raises further issues in leading a discussion.

are right answers, and the leader will have worked out where the discussion should end up. At the end of the night the group should be saying: "God has spoken to us by his word. What should we do?" rather than "We sure had a fiery discussion tonight!"

The leader is not just a chairperson or facilitator. The goal is not just to create a permissive, open environment with free-wheeling debate. The leader is a Bible teacher, responsible for the conclusions drawn by the group.

Freedom: control inhibits discussion

What kills a discussion? One sure way is to create the sense that the group has to come up with the right answer. They can't really say what they like—they might be corrected. The process of discussion seems controlled and everyone becomes inhibited. Any actions that communicate evaluation, control, strategy or superiority reduce spontaneity and openness in discussion. For example, these are sure-fire conversation stoppers: saying an answer is wrong, refusing to discuss an issue, or saying "It's different in the Hebrew text".

There appears to be a tension between these two principles. On the one hand we want discussion to go somewhere; on the other, we can't afford to completely control discussion.

We have come to **the basic dilemma** in leading Bible discussions. The discussion method we have inherited is influenced by today's popular worldview, which says that no-one is wrong and everyone is at least a little bit right—there is truth in what everyone thinks. Discussions work well in this non-defensive, accepting climate where there is no particular predetermined answer or end point to which things are heading and the whole exercise is open-ended.

So, how do we run energetic, stimulating discussions on the Bible, and yet steer the group to clear conclusions about what God has revealed? The methods below will help us achieve this balance of freedom and control.

5.2 UNDER WHAT AUTHORITY?

One of the problems with the discussion method of Bible study is the reduced sense of sitting under the authority of God's word. In the larger congregation, under a good preacher, it is clear that the congregation is to submit to the word of God as it is declared week by week. But in small groups, because they tend to operate by discussion and consensus, the group can become its own authority. Even in discussion of the Bible, a consensus style turns the group into the judge of Scripture.

This approach is back-to-front. The group must have a sense that God is speaking through Scripture. Obedience is mandatory. Keep asking yourself: Am I leading the group to sit under the authority of God's word?

5.3 STRATEGY

Leading a group Bible study is like guiding a hike in the mountains. It requires:

1. **Leader preparation**
2. **Group member preparation**
3. **Getting it started**
4. **Keeping it going**
5. **Winding it up**

Like a discussion, leading a hike involves a balance of control and freedom. It is reprehensible for the leader not to be well prepared, with clear directions and resources to reach the final objective. Likewise, the party must be adequately prepared, although usually there will be within it various levels of expertise. During the hike, the leader will need to keep motivation high and be firm in pushing on toward the final destination. Whatever else happens, the leader needs to keep studying the map and checking the landmarks. The guide needs to keep control.

But this is a hike, not a forced march at double time with full pack and a sergeant barking orders! The group can set its own pace to some extent and stop at points of interest along the way. The new hikers can learn a lot from the old timers who often know the terrain even better than the leader. Sometimes, they would like to get off the beaten track and find a new way home. To enjoy the experience and to come back for more, they need a fair degree of freedom.

These are the main strategies in leading a discussion.

1. Leader preparation: plan thoroughly, but be flexible

The leader of a hiking party must prepare thoroughly, working out the final destination and how to get there, but adjusting the plan as the trek unfolds.

We have looked at the leader's preparation in training topic 4: *Preparing a Bible study*. The study leader needs clear teaching goals and a discussion package which takes the group on the journey toward the goals. But we need flexibility in using our plan, to minimize the control problem.

In many ways, discussions are more demanding for leaders than are monologues. In a monologue or 'set piece', you have prepared what you will say. You have complete control. In a discussion, you don't know what direction it will take. Good preparation means you will not be caught off guard, at least not all the time! For example, if you have anticipated the tricky parts in a passage or the controversial topics it might generate, when they come up in discussion, you will be ready to use them to get to your goals.

A certain subtlety and finesse is essential, because you can't be sure what issues will arise in conversation. Rather than bulldozing on through your set questions like a quiz, deal with topics as they arise. The group then knows you are responding to their input. They are genuinely setting the agenda. They are more open to think and learn at the time they raise the issue, even if it was at the end of your page of questions. Deal with their true interests, not just yours.

2. Group member preparation: establish the ground rule

To make the most of the hike, each member of the party needs to prepare. Getting out the maps, knowing the track, anticipating points of interest and possible obstacles will all add value to the excursion.

The discussion and learning process will be much more efficient if each member does some preparation before the study. Discuss this ground rule up front—best of all, as a condition of joining the group. The type of preparation you request will depend on the maturity and educational background of the group. Avoid calling this preparation 'homework' or 'assignments' when in an adult Growth Group, because these words can revive too many negative memories of school detentions, report cards and so on.

You don't need to ask for massive amounts of preparation, maybe just two or three interesting questions to get the group thinking about the passage before they arrive. This will give momentum to the discussion. It only works if everyone does it, otherwise you have some group members way ahead of the rest, who may not bother catching up.

An important hint: don't use the preparation questions to start your discussion. The tendency then is for the group to read their answers, which does very little to generate enthusiasm.

3. Getting it started

You are more likely to get to the top of the mountain if the enthusiasm is high at base camp. If the climbers are dragging their heels from the first step, it's going to be uphill all the way.

Your launching question[2] gets the group moving and then you guide them up the hill. To try another metaphor, it's like dropping a bomb in the room—in the subsequent chaos, the group works to put the pieces together to make a new dwelling.

The launching question has to open up the discussion. It should create healthy tension by raising a topic that is relevant to the passage and the group and by raising many possible answers. The group is then caught up in the discussion, because tension has to be relieved, not unlike the plot of a good story.

In fact, the short story is yet another metaphor for leading a discussion. The introduction has to engage the reader by posing a dilemma for the main characters, and the body of the story proceeds to unravel the dilemma. The tension of the dilemma needs to be maintained until the stage where all the threads of the plot come together and there is a final resolution.

4. Keeping it going

Starting out fresh and keen for a long hike is one thing; trudging on through the late afternoon to reach camp for the night is a whole new challenge. What strategies keep the group working on the text and reaching conclusions? How does the leader avoid breaking into sermon mode?

---

2   For an explanation of the 'launching question', see training topic 4: *Preparing a Bible study.*

More questions

The role of the leader is to ask questions, not answer them. Even when the group asks questions, the leader ought not answer them. Instead, ask another question. The principle is: don't tell them what they can work out for themselves.

When you give answers you relieve tension, the adrenalin stops and so does discussion. At this point, you need to use your other prepared questions: observation, correlation, interpretation, summary, application.

There are other guiding or probing questions. 'Probing' is the best description of the role of the leader at this stage. The aim is to get the group thinking through ideas, challenging, correcting, refining or dismissing what has been said so far. The group has to do the work, not the leader giving them the bottom line. Ask questions of the following types:

- Extending: What can you add to that? Could you explain that more fully?
- Clarifying: What do you mean by that? Could you re-phrase that statement?
- Justifying: What reason can you give for that? Can you explain that from the passage?
- Re-directing: What do others think? Mary, what do you think?
- Reflecting: What I think you're saying is ... Is that right?

Welcome pauses

Don't be afraid of silence. Pauses are essential in a good discussion. They provide time to think, to formulate responses and to maintain the tension. As leaders, we tend to be vacuum-fillers, blurting out anything to end the silence, usually because we are insecure about how the discussion is going.

Value every contribution, but not equally

Every input to the discussion is valuable, both to the individual because it required thought, and to the group because they have to think in order to respond. Showing genuine interest in every contribution is a key to getting high participation.

This means:

- we can't always be thinking about our next comment or question
- our body language should indicate interest, by leaning forward and making eye contact

- we should use the actual words and expressions of members to show that we have taken their ideas on board
- we need to be enthusiastic about their input to the discussion.

Use the group input to build the discussion and unravel the issues. But *discrimination* is needed: each contribution does not have the same value. There are two specific cases where leaders need to be discriminating in responding to input, which we look at now.

Handling wrong or inadequate answers

If the leader jumps in and corrects every inadequate answer, there will soon be no discussion. Who is going to stick their neck out when it is sure to get the chop?

Although there is not always one right answer to a question, some comments will be dead wrong, because we are discussing biblical truth. Other answers will be on the right track, but inadequate. Others will be spot on. If the leader warmly accepts every contribution as 'gospel', there will be no credibility to the leadership. Once again, the issue is the tension between freedom and control. What are some strategies for handling error?

- We can ignore the error for the moment, hoping that the penny will drop further down the track.
- We can ask the group to respond, hoping that other members will move the discussion closer to the truth.
- We can probe further, saying "That's partly right, but there's more to it" or asking "Do you mean ...?" or "If that is true, then what about ...?"

Handling the right answer

Handling the right answer can be harder than dealing with error. Once the group sees that the answer is right or the issue is resolved, the discussion dies because the tension has been resolved. If they sense a positive judgment by the leader, that's game, set and match. If the leader thinks it was right, there seems to be no point going further.

Often someone gets the point quite early in the discussion. The leader has to stay neutral at this stage and avoid any evaluating comments or gestures. Little comments like 'good', 'fine' or nodding indicate approval, and everyone switches off. You might just grunt and wait for other responses or elicit these with a question like "What do others think?" The group will complain when they reach this same conclusion twenty minutes later: "Fred said that ages ago!" True, but only Fred understood it then. Now they all do.

Keep interacting with the text of the Bible

There may be all kinds of interesting diversions and sidetracks on a hike, but to get to the destination you need to follow the map.

In a Bible study, our tendency is to get absorbed in ideas and generalities rather than to wrestle with the meaning of the Bible. We would rather speculate on all kinds of topics that interest us, instead of doing the harder work of Bible reading. It's a very common problem. A group starts by studying Colossians chapter 2, but ends up making general comments about the Sabbath without connecting the discussion to Bible passages.

If the Bibles are closed and superfluous to the discussion, we have lost the plot. As leaders we can draw the group back into Bible study by asking a new question about the passage before us, for example: "From verse 17, in what way is the Sabbath a shadow of the things that were to come?" Keep coming back to the Bible itself.

Encourage the group to ask questions

One of the reasons for hiking in a pack is the value and enjoyment of interaction as well as keeping each other on course.

It is a great moment in a discussion group when the leader slips into the background and the group 'goes solo'. The leader has not lost control, but all around the room members are interacting and the group has gathered its own momentum. It is moving toward the right conclusions on its own, without being led by the hand. It is most exciting when members are at the same time looking after each other by listening to each contribution and asking further questions.

5. Winding it up

Getting to the destination together, with everyone still on track, is a good result on a hike. There are a number of less satisfactory endings to the expedition: everyone wandering around in the bush for a few days, or ending up in the wrong town, or leaving one or two behind. These disasters are all variations on a theme. It's called Getting Lost.

Winding up the discussion is the art of not getting lost. At the end of the discussion you want to:

- reinforce the central truths and supporting truths from the passage
- highlight the relevant applications
- pray together about these applications.

Two problems arise in doing this, both related to freedom and control:

- Your summary should reflect the group discussion, not your prepared study. If you just give your conclusions that you worked out beforehand, the group feels duped. You played a game with them, never intending to take on board their input. Sometimes the group's conclusions won't match yours. It is a challenge to give a summary which captures the discussion in full colour.
- The act of summarizing suppresses further inquiry. Everything gets tied up neatly; we don't feel the need to think any more; tension is relieved. That's not how we want the group to feel at the end of a discussion. We want the group to be still climbing the wall to get to the truth. Then they will return to the group, or maybe not leave till the wee hours of the morning!

  But, we have to come to some conclusions about God and his word. There has to be a sense that God has taught us and we must act. If we leave it all up in the air, we have succumbed to relativism, where every opinion contains some truth. Bible study can't end that way.

One approach

Here is a suggested way to wind the discussion up, which seeks to maintain the balance of freedom and control:

- Summarize what the group has agreed upon thus far. There may not be complete consensus but summarize the overwhelming trend.
- If the conclusions are true to the Bible, draw out the applications and pray.
- Identify where the group has disagreed, or where unanswered questions remain. This can provide fuel for further enquiry. It may not hurt to identify the dissenters. If the group conclusions don't seem to represent the text at hand, you may need to do more study, both in the group and privately.
- Don't become distressed trying to get everyone to agree on every issue.

They will grow in understanding and sort out their thinking over time. Over a few months, you will see growth. Permitting group members to hold and express different views is a prerequisite for growth. As they defend their ideas and compare them with biblical truth, they will be opened up to learning and change.

This approach resolves the dilemma: the group discussion is summarized with integrity, the group is confronted with clear conclusions from the passage and the sense of enquiry is not totally evaporated.

5.4 FOUR WARNINGS

1. Don't preach on your hobby horses

This is a sure way to kill discussion and usually distorts the main thrust of the Bible passage.

2. Don't avoid controversy and conflict

Not knowing how to regain control and draw some valid conclusions may be frightening, but when people get churned up, good progress is often around the corner. The conflict can indicate that they are questioning their beliefs and values, which is a precondition for learning and change. And it's not boring. Instead of avoiding controversy, welcome it.

3. Don't pretend you know everything

You don't and you don't need to. It is great for the group to see you struggle with understanding the Bible. It prevents you from being the guru with all the answers. Get members to do some research on a difficult topic and report back to the group. That's much more motivating and edifying than hearing you pretend you know it all.

4. Don't answer your own questions

This is a symptom of leader insecurity. It causes discussion to devolve into a monologue with a rhetorical flavour. It does little to develop the group.

Answers about questions

Questions are the life force of discussions. Asking the right question at the right time is the art of leading a discussion. It is true for all forms of enquiry: asking the right question is a prerequisite for getting the right answer.

6.1 WHY ASK QUESTIONS?

John Milton Gregory in *The Seven Laws of Teaching*[1] describes teaching and learning:

Teaching is arousing and using the pupil's mind to grasp the desired thought or to master the desired act.

Learning is thinking into one's own understanding a new idea or truth or working into habit a new art or skill.

The purpose of asking questions is to accomplish this teaching and learning. Questions stimulate thought: arousing, clarifying, guiding, analyzing.

---

1   JM Gregory, *The Seven Laws of Teaching*, Baker, Grand Rapids, 1972 (1884).

6.2 TYPES OF QUESTIONS

There are two broad types of discussion questions.

Prepared questions

These are the launching, observation, correlation, interpretation, summary and application questions we looked at in training topic 4: *Preparing a Bible study*. Although prepared beforehand, they are to be used in a flexible way, responding to what happens in the group rather than asking them in a rigid, systematic way. To the group, they may often appear to be spontaneous.

Facilitating questions

These are the spontaneous questions that facilitate the discussion, keeping it moving forward. They are important for building the habit of listening attentively to each other. We looked at some of these in training topic 5: *Leading a Bible study*—extending, clarifying, justifying, re-directing and reflecting questions.

6.3 A GOOD QUESTION

Here are some characteristics of a good question.

Open-ended, not closed

Good questions tend to be open-ended. They require a thoughtful response, rather than a simple 'Yes' or 'No'. Open-ended questions often start with the words 'What', 'How' or 'Why'. Closed questions, in contrast, limit the possible responses of those listening.

Open question: "What does it mean to continue to live in Christ?"
Closed question: "What are the four ways to continue to live in Christ?"
Closed question: "Is God concerned that we continue to live in Christ?"

Doesn't anticipate the answer

Questions should not be leading. Questions which lead the group in a certain direction won't achieve the purpose of making the group think.

Poor question: "Jesus was God, wasn't he?"

Simple, not double-barrelled

Questions that have two or more parts confuse the group because they do not know where to start their answers. Each question should address one issue.

Poor question: "What does it mean to continue to live in Christ, why is it important and are you doing it?"

Concise rather than complex

Questions should not need further elaboration. They should suit the group in word choice, in the level of the ideas involved, and in the amount of background knowledge required to answer.

Poor question: "In Paul's eloquent discourse on the profundity of Christological soteriology, what is his view of traditional ceremonial religion for justification and sanctification?'

Better question: "What's wrong with keeping rules?"

The games people play

Members of a Growth Group adopt different roles which affect the functioning of the whole group. They are often unaware of the roles they take—they are just being themselves. However, they are playing a highly sophisticated 'game', a pattern of conducting relationships which has been developed over many years. Identifying the various 'games' operating within a group allows the leader to manage individual group members.

7.1 CONSTRUCTIVE ROLES

Some roles are constructive and need to be encouraged and reinforced by the leader:

- The Peacemaker: resolves disputes
- The Focuser: keeps to the task
- The Encourager: positive about others
- The Sympathizer: draws out people's feelings
- The Initiator: gets the ball rolling
- The Summarizer: draws together the argument
- The Humorist: lightens the moment

- The Devil's Advocate: sharpens people's thinking
- The Socializer: organizes the social life of the group

7.2 DESTRUCTIVE ROLES

Other roles are destructive and need monitoring as possible causes of group malfunction. These are worth looking at in some detail, along with some strategies for coping with the problems such roles cause, and trying to eliminate them.

1. The Onlooker

This describes the non-contributor, or the person who has minimal participation in the group. In a quiet group they can cause problems, especially if there are too many Onlookers. Alternatively, the Onlooker may be the product of other forces at work in the group, such as anger and aggression. In this case, it is the aggressive members who need attention more than the silent ones.

Strategies:
- Direct clear, simple questions to them if they are secure enough in the group to cope with having to answer.
- Respond eagerly to anything they say or do, acknowledging their response with praise, if appropriate, to boost their confidence. The leader's body language—such as eye contact or leaning toward the group—will communicate warmth and interest.
- Be alert as to when they are trying to enter the discussion.
- If they are intimidated by others, deal with this problem.
- If they are bored, work out why and discover their interests. Ask for their advice and comments: "Vera, you have had some experience with ... would you tell us what you found?"
- Get all members to write some answers to a question and read them out themselves, thus involving Onlookers to the same extent as other members.
- Sometimes use smaller sub-groups to reduce the nervousness of addressing a big group.

2. The Monopolizer

We have all met these people. They can act as if no-one else exists in their world, and they just love the sound of their own voice. Their dominance is often a mask for their own insecurity. Some are simply born ramblers.

Strategies:
- Reiterate agreed ground rules, such as helping others to join the discussion.
- Sit yourself next to them to reduce eye contact which tends to invite participation.
- Give specific instructions in your questions. For example: "I want those who have not said anything before to answer this question."
- Interrupt the Monopolizer in the middle of a long speech. For example: "You have obviously thought through the issue, let's see what others think." or "We have heard your ideas on this topic, Joe, let's move on to discuss ..."
- When they pause for breath, thank them by acknowledging their point, and move on.
- Talk to them privately about the problem and suggest they serve others by drawing them into the discussion.

3. The Sidetracker

The Sidetracker arrives every week with a bag full of red herrings. They just cannot stay focused on the topic or task. Unfortunately, sometimes the red herring is more interesting than the set discussion and this poses a problem for the group and for you.

Strategies:
- The leader doesn't have to respond to all input. Simply let some comments pass.
- Ask new questions to divert the discussion back to the topic.
- Acknowledge the sidetrack and suggest it be picked up over supper.
- Some apparent sidetracks are worth pursuing, when they are important topics or will lead toward the discussion goals.
- Privately raise the problem and suggest they serve the rest of the group by not raising side issues.

4. The Clown

The group clown can be an asset. He or she relieves tension and sets a happy tone to the group. The Clown becomes a problem if they are attracting attention to themselves and distracting the group, or if the humour is inappropriate.

Strategies:
- Don't always laugh.

5. The Expert

Some group members appear to be very knowledgeable on certain subjects (in some cases, *all* topics). Is this merely their perception or is it true?

Strategies:
- Give them a suitable task, such as a five minute talk, allowing the group to benefit from, and test, the Expert's knowledge.
- Make them an ally in running the group; ask them to give feedback to the leaders.

6. The Fighter

The Fighter is argumentative and may be aggressive. They do have the positive effect of stirring up debate, because they are dissatisfied with cliches and the party line. But they intimidate others.

Strategies:
- Win some arguments to demonstrate their fallibility.
- Avoid being drawn into heated debate and losing the plot.
- Privately, point out the negative effect they have on the group.

7. The Chatterer

Chatterers conduct little conversations with their neighbour, distracting everyone. Sometimes they are chatting about the discussion topic, sometimes about unrelated matters.Whatever the subject, their mouths are open more than they are closed.

Strategies:

- Pause and let everyone listen. This is a gentle way of drawing attention to the fact that they are disruptive.
- Draw them into the discussion by asking their opinion: "We would all be interested in your comments, Bob." Try not to be sarcastic about this; be genuine.

7.3 GENERAL STRATEGIES

There are general strategies for handling the different roles people play in a Growth Group:

- Work out the positive as well as negative effects of the roles various people adopt in your group.
- Work out why certain people adopt the roles they do.
- Ask: is this person giving just a one-off performance or is their behaviour a set pattern?

Praying in growth groups

If there is one sure-fire prayer point in small groups, it's praying that God will make us more prayerful! Everyone believes in prayer; everyone recognizes that we need to pray more; but everyone has trouble making it a priority. Put it down to the bustle of modern life, or simply to sinful, independent hearts—either way, we can always find something which is more pressing than speaking to God in prayer.

Getting Christian groups praying is not about suggesting techniques which, like diets, tend to last for a few days before we break them, feel like failures and give up altogether. Instead, we focus upon enduring ideas which should pervade our prayer life.

8.1 PRAYER RUTS

Most Christian groups pray. Most Christian groups easily drift into prayer ruts. Our times of prayer become hurried intercessions, a quick vote of thanks at the end of the Bible study, prayers for the sick or 'those who aren't with us', or general prayers for more love and peace. Of course, these are all great things to pray for, but we usually end up praying for them *by default*, because we don't put in the time and effort to think about what to pray.

Most groups find it easier to do Bible study (or have supper) than to pray. Prayer gets reduced to a minimum, sometimes included only to relieve our guilt about it.

8.2 PRAYER WARRIORS

Devote yourselves to prayer, being watchful and thankful.

COLOSSIANS 4:2

We want our groups to love praying, to long to pray to God. Our group meetings can be training grounds for great prayer warriors. What is it that will help our group to be devoted to prayer? Here are a few ideas:

- **The example of leaders:** You must first address prayer in your own life. The group will see whether you are a prayer warrior or a prayer wimp. Enough said.
- **Give prayer priority in group time:** You may need to be creative in order to achieve this. Occasionally, devote the entire meeting to prayer. Start your meeting with prayer, instead of leaving it until the end. Pray at several different points during the meeting. Pray spontaneously as issues arise from discussion.
- **Keep track of the group's prayer concerns:** Some groups use a 'prayer diary', so they can look back to what they have prayed about and write down specific events, people and occasions to pray for in the future. It is a very helpful aid to memory.
- **Be confident in God through Christ:** Ultimately, this is what drives us to pray. It is the truth of the gospel—that we are lost on our own, but have entered into relationship with God through Christ—which will sustain us in prayer. We need to keep teaching the gospel. It reveals the love of the Father in his Son for his people. If we doubt that God cares for us, and hears and responds to our prayers, we will never pray. We need to recall that "He who did not spare his own Son, but gave him up for us all—how will he not also, along with him, graciously give us all things" (Rom 8:32).

8.3 CHRISTIAN PRAYER

There are numerous prayer techniques being promoted in churches which are not true Christian prayer. The Christian form of prayer comes from the gospel of our Lord Jesus Christ, the Son of the Father. We pray:

- to the Father
- through the Son (on the basis of his death)
- in and by the Spirit
- using ordinary language.

It is worth carefully modelling this in our groups, and not allowing any special techniques. There is no human technique for prayer. Prayer is available to those who trust Jesus. Believers have marvellous access to the Father through him. The current trends towards meditating in prayer, listening to God in prayer, having dialogue with God, journalling, imagining and prayer dreams have moved away from the gospel basis of prayer.

8.4 EXPANDING OUR CONCERNS

Our prayers are often of a totally different character to the prayers of the Bible. For example, look at the prayers in the following passages:

2 Samuel 7:18-29

Matthew 6:5-15

Colossians 1:3-14

Note the concerns of these prayers: the grand purposes of God; the salvation of Israel through David's dynasty; the growth of the gospel and of believers; the coming of the Kingdom of God; the renown of God. In short, they are God-centred, not self-centred, prayers. They are full of thanks to God, rehearsing his holiness and saving power and asking him to fulfil his plans to save the world.

Paul sets an agenda for prayer meetings in 1 Timothy 2:1-7. We are to pray for everyone, with the focus upon godly living and the salvation of all. Of course, we can bring our personal needs to God in prayer (see 1 Pet 5:7; Matt 6:25-34). By bringing all matters to God, even the minor details of our lives, we express faith in God's rule over all things. God has committed himself to provide and care for us.

8.5 COLLECTING PRAYER POINTS

The old routine of collecting prayer points is a mixed blessing. It is good to hear others' concerns so that we can pray very specifically—it is one of the key ways we express our love for each other. But this routine does present some problems. It takes a lot of time, and the actual praying gets tacked on the end of the discussion. It can become repetitive, with the same issues being raised every week. It can be difficult at certain stages of the group's existence for people to be honest and open with their prayer requests. The main problem, however, with sharing prayer points is that it promotes self-centred praying.

Beyond our personal concerns, what should the group be praying about? Our prayers should reflect God's purposes in his world, so we should pray for:

- **Gospel preaching:** The group might adopt a missionary or evangelist for whom they can pray, as they keep track of his or her activities and needs.
- **Unbelievers:** Pray for the salvation of your unbelieving friends and families. Pray more widely for the conversion of those in positions of power, of people who have a public profile, or even of neighbours whom you don't know.
- **The growth of the church in godliness:** Pray for your church's programs and plans. Perhaps adopt a particular ministry, such as Sunday School, and pray for it for a period.
- **Our own growth in godliness:** This is an important focus for the group. Pray about your responses to the sermons you hear. Pray about the Bible studies you do in the group, that God will help you to apply what you learn to your mind and behaviour. Most groups need help in doing this, lest they drift into their own concerns rather than God's concerns, as expressed in the Bible passage. We need to learn to pray with 'open Bibles', rather than forgetting what we have just studied as we start our time of prayer.

8.6 THE GROUP DYNAMICS OF PRAYER

It can be hard to get everyone in a group to pray out loud, especially when the group is quite new and people are not yet comfortable with each other. How can we make this easier for each other?

Leading in prayer

When we pray with others, we are not only praying to God, we are also leading others in prayer. This is true in any Christian context, such as conferences, committees and church. We must be conscious of others, not in order to impress them, but to serve them. Here are some practical tips on serving people in prayer:

- Use the plural pronouns 'we' and 'our'. This signals that we are all praying, not just the person speaking.
- Say short prayers, so that everyone can maintain attention.
- Avoid jargon or complicated expressions; use language that everyone in the group will understand.
- Don't switch into an unnatural 'prayer mode'. Use your normal voice and keep a normal posture.

Form smaller groups

Reducing your group size into twos or threes for praying can lower people's anxieties and allow them to pray more openly. Single sex prayer groups can have the same effect.

Formulating prayers

When time is spent discussing what we want to pray, people are often more confident and willing to pray. A sense of unity in prayer is developed, making it easier for people honestly to say 'Amen' to each prayer. Discussing and formulating prayers before praying need not make praying a formality; it simply brings the group together in their support of the prayer.

8.7 PRAYER PARTNERS

You might wish to form 'prayer partnerships' within your group, where small groups of people regularly pray together. This tends to build more prayer into group life, as well as deepening some of the friendships in the group. There are endless possibilities for how such a partnership might operate. Here are but a few suggestions:

- Pray together during group meeting time.
- Pray together during the week, outside the group time.
- Pray for each other during the week, without meeting together.
- Change prayer partners every few weeks or months.

Gospel growth through growth groups

9.1 LOOKING INWARDS

Christian groups can become highly introverted, focusing on their own needs. Minority groups in society tend to withdraw into ghettos to find safety and comfort with other members of the same 'tribe'. It is a natural instinct for self-preservation in a world which is hostile or indifferent to the Lord.

Christian groups tend to become emotional support groups, the energy of the group being directed toward those with problems. We all have problems all the time and these problems tend to set the group's agenda.[1] One by-product of problem-focused groups is their inability to have an impact outside the group.

9.2 LOOKING OUTWARDS

Growth Groups can't afford to be introverted. It is contrary to their very nature. The group has been created by the word of the gospel, drawing the group's members to Christ and to each other. How can they *not* become a

---

1   See training topic 3: *Pitfalls for Growth Groups* for a more detailed discussion of this issue.

vehicle for communicating this message to the world?

What, then, is the mission of Growth Groups beyond itself?

We see something of the answer in our study of Colossians. In Colossians 1, we see that God is working through the preaching of the gospel. This gospel is bearing fruit and growing around the world. This growth is seen in the Colossians through their faith in Jesus, their love for other Christians and their hope in heaven. This gospel growth comes through God and his human agents as they bring the gospel to others. In chapter 4, Paul expects the group at Colossae to be involved in gospel growth in three ways:

- praying for gospel preachers
- being thoughtful about relationships with unbelievers
- speaking graciously but firmly of their Christian belief.

9.3 GROWTH GROUPS AS EVANGELISTIC TEAMS

Growth Groups facilitate teamwork in evangelism in several ways.

Overcoming fear

It is more comfortable inside the ghetto. Our fellow tribe members understand and accept us. When we become evangelists—moving out of the ghetto to invite others to join it—we are not popular. Evangelism also presents a communication problem. We want to tell people of the gracious loving Father who has given up his Son to make them his children. But evangelists are seen as narrow-minded, bigoted, moralistic ratbags infringing on other's civil rights. Who wants to be tarred with this brush?

Working together in evangelism helps to overcome this problem. It puts some steel in our souls as we pray, go on some gospel forays together and patch up each other's wounds. We can keep each other going when the response to our efforts is slow or hostile.

Training in evangelism

In Growth Groups we can train each other in taking opportunities, communicating the gospel and answering objections to faith. We can use the group context to learn skills for evangelizing, and for practising our gospel presentations with each other. It is an ideal place to discuss commonly raised questions about Christianity and dig into the Scriptures to find where these questions might be answered.

Demonstrating the gospel

In a sense, Growth Groups are a visual aid for the gospel of reconciliation. The way we conduct relationships within the group, modelling our behaviour on God himself, is distinctive and very attractive to the outsider.

When people see Christians relating to each other, they ought to be envious. Christians have just as many problems as the rest of the world, but fewer ulcers. We enjoy relationships more, including marriage, because we know how to forgive rather than seek revenge. We are not racist, sexist, ageist, homophobic or elitist. We work hard, using honest scales (Prov 11:1, 16:11). People are more important to us than organizations and bureaucracy. The only thing that bothers us about being poor is being a burden to others. If this sounds like fantasy, it shouldn't. It is a biblical description of what the Christian life should be like.

Exposing unbelievers to Christian relationships confronts them and opens them up to the gospel, which has so obviously given birth to new creatures.

Titus 2:5, 8, 10 expounds the importance of Christian behaviour in evangelism:

> *So that no one will malign the word of God ... so that those who oppose you may be ashamed because they have nothing bad to say about us ... so that in every way they will make the teaching about God our Saviour attractive.*

Complementing personalities in evangelism

We all have strengths and weaknesses in communicating the faith to others. Some of us are natural extroverts and love talking to anyone about anything, including the news of Jesus. Some like an argument and enjoy the push and shove of religious debate. Others are less articulate, but are very loving in good deeds. These differences in personality can all be put to good use in evangelism. There are, however, some skills which everyone can use—we can all learn how to invite someone to an evangelistic meeting.

The diversity of Christian groups makes for great teamwork and reduces the unwarranted guilty feelings of those who don't have the personality of a Christian chat-show host. After all, different people will be receptive to different styles of evangelism.

Group bonding

There is nothing like working at the gospel enterprise to build group unity and trust. The petty personality differences that might otherwise disrupt a group pale into insignificance in the face of heaven and hell. Evangelism is a great way to bond a group together, as you share in such a significant endeavour.

Gospel reality, not theory

One of the benefits of evangelistic effort through Growth Groups is that the group is faced squarely with the reality of the gospel. In trying to reach others, the big issues of heaven and hell, how God saves and who God saves are on the agenda. This often throws up doubts and confusion in Christian group members, which can then be addressed. In a group which is not evangelizing, issues can be blurred and the sharp edge of the gospel blunted. The group will better grasp Christian truth and its eternal implications when they are seeing these realities work out in evangelism.

9.4 EVANGELISM IN THE CONSTITUTION

Evangelism needs to be spelt out as a purpose of the group in its very 'constitution'. Along with Christian growth, gospel growth is at the heart of any Christian gathering. Bible Study, prayer and evangelistic effort are the three basic activities of a Growth Group, but if evangelism is just tacked on as an afterthought, it won't happen.

There are **two ways** to build evangelism into the founding constitution of the Growth Group.

1. Evangelize group contacts

In forming the group, agree together to reach out with the gospel to your relatives, friends and contacts. To accomplish this you might choose some of the strategies in 9.5 below.

2. Set a target group

In forming the group, agree together to evangelize a particular target group which is accessible to your group members. Aim for a target group which your members can relate to, based on geography, age, social class, ethnicity, work or social patterns.

Some examples of target groups:

- A workplace where a group of Christians form a Growth Group to reach colleagues.
- A school, college or university where students plan the evangelization of the campus.
- A group of 10 could join a sporting, fitness or recreational club to slowly build relationships which lead to the gospel.
- There may be a few Christians living in close proximity in a neighbourhood who could reach common friends.
- Christian parents in a school environment could reach other parents.
- Christians from a common ethnic background could team together.
- Your group could be part of the wider church strategy by following up contacts through church meetings, baptisms, weddings and funerals.

In fact, members could choose to join your group because they want to be part of a team reaching this target group. In some cases, such as ethnic evangelism, the group leaders might choose particular members because of their affinity with the target group.

Instead of tacking on a bit of evangelism to the group activities, in this way it becomes central to the mission of the group. It sees itself as an evangelistic team and its agenda is strongly influenced by this missionary purpose.

Adopt an evangelist or ministry

As well as the group working at evangelism, they need to learn to be committed to wider gospel work. This can begin with regular prayer for your area, city, nation and particular countries.[2] A further step in learning to support gospel work is for the group to 'adopt' a ministry or evangelist, swapping photos, tapes and letters and so making a strong commitment to a particular work. It may be that you pray regularly for a particular ministry in your church, such as the Sunday school. You might ask teachers to visit your group to talk about their class.

However it is done, this sort of support for gospel work enhances the group's sense of the great mission of evangelism.

9.5 DEVELOPING THE STRATEGIES

There are simple and straightforward ways to ensure that evangelism is high on your group's agenda:

- Meet regularly for Bible study, prayer and friendship.
- Start praying for everyone you are reaching, whether individual contacts or a common target group. Make up a group prayer list of every unbeliever you want to bring to Christ.
- Think together about the people you want to evangelize, in order to better understand them and to sort out the best ways of communicating Christ to them. Consider questions such as:

  Who is this person and what makes them tick?

  What are their beliefs and values?

  What influences have shaped them?

  What motivates them?

  What persuades them something is true: logic, people or experience?

  What is their religious background?

  What do they know about Christianity?

---

2   See P Johnstone, *Operation World*, 6th edn, Paternoster, Carlisle, 2001. *Operation World*, a handbook of the state of gospel growth around the world, is a useful prayer and information resource.

What is their attitude to Christianity?

What are the big implications for them if they follow Jesus?

- Work out how you can make a positive contribution to the lives of your contacts or target group: providing material needs; organizing social events; remembering birthdays.
- Aim to get into 'meaningful conversation' about anything other than the gospel with each person. Jumping from light banter about the weekend into evangelistic conversations is quite a social hurdle! If you are comfortable in other types of meaningful conversation, the gospel will arise more naturally.
- Work at naturally letting individuals know you are a Christian.
- Invite unbelievers to as many social events with the Growth Group as possible. Make these events purely social—no evangelism. These might be dinner parties, outings or sports—whatever suits them. The aims are to let them see that Christians aren't aliens, and to make it easier to invite them to evangelistic activities. They are often quite surprised that such a group exists and amazed by the style of relationships.
- Work out ways of introducing the gospel with each person in private conversation (not at the social events).
- Put on a group evangelistic event that is appropriate for your contacts.

9.6 TRAINING THE GROUP

Throughout the life of the group, there are marvellous opportunities for training group members in how to communicate the gospel. When you are active in evangelism, it becomes clear that training is helpful.

There are training courses available which could be incorporated into the group program,[3] but here are some other ideas for training activities:
- Discuss how to pray for the unsaved and for evangelism generally.
- Discuss subjects such as overcoming fear and turning conversations to the gospel.

---

3   See appendix I.

- Do some 'cold-contact evangelism' at local parks, shopping centres or doorknocking, to develop evangelistic skills.
- Do some newcomer visitation under the supervision of your church leaders.
- At the end of Bible studies, discuss how you could teach the passage to non-Christians.
- Use Bible studies to raise apologetic issues. In this way, the group learns how to use the Bible to answer objections.
- Debrief members about their efforts and offer encouragement and advice.
- Invite a skilled, enthusiastic evangelist to speak to the group.
- Discuss how to use evangelistic meetings: who to invite and how to do it; how to make sure they get there; looking after them during and after the meeting; follow up.
- Discuss how to make unbelievers comfortable when they come to your activities. For example, what should you do about saying grace at a dinner? Should you provide alcohol?

9.7 SHOULD UNBELIEVERS JOIN THE GROUP?

If we are aiming to spread the gospel through the group, why not invite non-Christians to join it? That would seem a natural extension to making the group outward-looking and bringing the gospel to others. It can actually work very well if certain conditions are met:
- The group needs to agree with this step. It may have been part of the original plan for the group or a development that has been talked through.
- The group needs to think through beforehand how to handle newcomers, so the members are welcoming and wise with them. They need to understand the difficulties in joining an existing group, the tendencies to gang up on those with alternative views and for the discussion to centre on the outsiders.
- The joining unbelievers need to agree to the ground rules of the group. It is a group for Bible reading and prayer, not for debating every possible objection to Christianity. If they are willing to try and understand the Bible with us, it will work. They don't have to agree with all we say, but

they must be willing to join in the group activity of analyzing the Bible. When the group prays, they can just listen to our prayers or join in. The success of such a venture depends very much on the unbeliever's disposition—whether they are seeking God or seeking to disrupt.

Advantages

It can be enormously helpful for unbelievers to learn to read the Bible with Christians and to see ordinary people struggling with faith, love and obedience. It can dispel many myths about Christianity.

It can also be a great learning experience for the Christians. Their often cliched answers to questions are challenged and jargon has to be explained. They observe each other interacting with unbelievers—with their personalities and their questions.

Disadvantages

A group which decides to welcome unbelievers is never the same again. Even though the members may be enthusiastic and well prepared, there are, at least initially, inhibitions. There is a sense of having to perform for the unbelievers. This can be overcome as Christians realize that non-Christians benefit much more when they see the doubts, fears and sinfulness of supposedly holy people.

Another strategy

Instead of unbelievers joining the Growth Group, some of your group members could spawn a new group at another time, especially for outsiders. This can be a motivating project for the whole group—they seek to invite their friends to come to this evangelistic group. It might be a short term group which meets for four or five weeks to explain the basics of the gospel.[4] Those who are converted or on the way might then like to join the Growth Group.

---

4   See appendix I for evangelistic Bible studies that could be used in this enquirers' group.

Leading for growth

10.1 THE MYTH OF THE LEADERLESS GROUP

Why should we have leaders of Growth Groups? Why not let the groups run themselves?

There is a popular view in Christian small groups that a designated leader is unnecessary and a positive disadvantage. In these 'leaderless' groups, all members are expected to provide leadership in different ways. There seems to be a contemporary fear that designated leadership stifles the gifts of the group members, and that the responsibility of running the group is too much for one person. It is thought that members will have a greater sense of group ownership and motivation in a leaderless group because they can shape its destiny.

These are legitimate concerns which we will address by looking at what leadership is and how it is exercised.

At the pragmatic level, there are two realities to recognize at the outset. Firstly, there is no such thing as a group without a leader. The leaderless group is a myth. Any form of human society or grouping will generate its own leadership if none is designated. Even with a recognized leader, the group will often produce an alternative—it's known as a coup! If there is no appointed leader, someone or several people will lead in some way, perhaps quite unobtrusively, perhaps overtly. Someone will fill the vacuum and set the directions and policies of the group. In Growth Groups, where we have specific Christian aims, it is negligent not to appoint suitable leaders.

Secondly, leaderless groups are unstable. They tend to lack consistency in direction and program and are more likely to self-destruct because of a loss of motivation and unresolved tensions.

10.2 THE RISE OF THE DICTATOR

A very different problem with authority has resulted in a trend towards highly authoritarian small group leaders. We have seen them in some house churches and breakaway small groups. Often, these groups commence because of a strong leader with strong reactions to the status quo. Group members develop intense loyalty to this leader and his vision and, in the end, his leadership is not tested by Scripture. Some of these leaders become guru figures who require from group members obedience to very specific demands.

10.3 SHEPHERDS, SERVANTS AND STEWARDS

These are the most common images of leadership used in the Bible.

Shepherd

The Father is the Shepherd who will seek out one lost sheep (Matt 18:12-14). The Son, Jesus, is also the Shepherd of his sheep. He protects the flock by laying down his life for them. He speaks in such a way that the sheep know and follow him and, as the good Shepherd, he guards the sheep from wolves (John 10:1-30; Mark 14:27; 1 Pet 2:25; Heb 13:20).

Following the model of their chief Shepherd, Christian leaders are also shepherds, leading the church by the truth of God's word and guarding the flock from wolves who teach falsehood (1 Pet 5:1-5; Acts 20:28; Eph 4:11; John 21:15-17).

Growth Group leaders are like shepherds—expendable. They give up their lives for the group. And they lead the group to salvation and maturity by teaching the Bible. The leader has no inherent authority over the group and the group is not its own authority. The sole authority is the word of God.

There is a common misperception that pastoral ministry is distinct from teaching ministry. Pastoral work is seen as caring for the people through activities such as visitation, counselling, baptisms and marriage. This is a false distinction with serious consequences. If the pastor doesn't teach the word of God, he is not leading the flock into salvation and security. He may have great people skills and provide superb service and advice but he is not shepherding the flock unless he is teaching the Bible. (NB. The word 'pastor' is another word for 'shepherd'.)

The Growth Group leader is much *more* than a facilitator, administrator or coordinator. Shepherd is a better description. The leader guides the group by teaching the word of God.

The leader doesn't have to do everything, because the members are to use their gifts to build up each other. However, the leader has an overall responsibility for where the group ends up in Christian understanding and thinking.

Servant

Ministers are servants and ministry is service. Our English Bible translations tend to use 'ministry' language, but the nature of ministry would be clearer if they used the normal word 'service'. 'Ministry' has come to have a kind of institutional meaning, instead of referring chiefly to the act of serving others.

When looking at the passages mentioned below, read 'service' for 'ministry' and 'servant' for 'minister'.

Jesus came as our servant, giving his life as a ransom. The One who is God himself and exalted above all others became a servant in his humiliation and death (Matt 20:28; Phil 2:6-11). For Jesus' disciples, the way to greatness is not by high office but by service (Matt 20:20-28).

All Christians are servants of God, instead of sin (Rom 6:22), servants of Christ (Rom 12:11, 14:18), and servants of one another (Gal 5:13; Eph 4:12).

Christian leaders are:

- servants of God (2 Cor 6:4)
- servants of God by teaching his people (1 Tim 4:6)
- servants of Christ by preaching the gospel (Acts 26:16; Rom 1:1; 1 Cor 4:1; Col 4:12, 13)
- servants of the gospel (Luke 1:2; Acts 6:1-4; Eph 3:7; Col 1:23)
- servants of God's people by preaching the gospel (1 Cor 9:19; 2 Cor 4:5, 5:18, 11:7-8; Col 1:7).

The aim of a Growth Group leader is to serve rather than be served. Leadership is not a means to position, status or personal fulfilment. In our self-centredness we can use ministry to promote ourselves and to get a thrill out of having authority. The group is then serving our desires and the whole exercise is muddled.

There are many ways in which a leader serves a group. In the end, service is an attitude of living for God and his people. Service is not about following a job description, but there is a primary service which a leader provides for the group—teaching the gospel. To bring the group into the knowledge and salvation of Christ is our highest calling as servants.

Steward

This image of Christian leaders derives from the manager or administrator entrusted with the affairs of the household. The primary characteristic of a steward is trustworthiness in the owner's eyes, expressed by faithfulness in doing his work.

The New American Standard Bible consistently uses 'stewardship' language in the the following passages. Paul is a steward of God and the gospel, and exercises this trust by preaching the gospel (1 Cor 4:1, 9:17; Col 1:25; Eph 3:2). Overseers are also stewards (Titus 1:7), as are all Christians in the faithful use of their gifts to serve each other (1 Pet 4:10).

As Growth Group leaders, what constitutes success? We could have all kinds of parameters to evaluate our leadership: numerical growth, spiritual growth, enthusiasm, regular attendance. However, the measure of success as stewards is our faithfulness in God's business. Have we held on tenaciously to the truth of the gospel against all attacks and taught this gospel to the group? We are not responsible for the final outcome in others, or how dynamic the group feels, but we must be trustworthy teachers of God's word.

10.4 WHO SHOULD LEAD?

Do you get the feeling that leaders have a big job? Do you want to bail out? It sounds more and more like you are going to be the pastor of a church. You thought you were just going to read the Bible and pray with a few friends once a week, and still keep your day job!

One of the reasons leaderless groups are popular is because leadership seems like a burdensome and demanding task. It is! Let's not pretend otherwise.

Growth Group leaders have the most important job amongst the volunteer workforce of a church. Let's think through how this is the case. If the church treasurer runs off with the weekly offering, the bank manager may be upset, but the congregation will remain Christians. If the songleader doesn't know anything written since the 16th century, the singing may be less than enthusiastic, but the members will still be Christians. If the church property committee chooses the wrong builder, it is unlikely to lead many off the straight and narrow path.

But leaders of Growth Groups have a direct impact on the spiritual life of the church. What goes on in those groups will shape the Christian thinking and living of its members. The Growth Group leader gets close to the group and has a lot of influence upon it.

So what qualifies a person to lead a Growth Group? From Paul's instructions to Timothy and Titus (1 Tim 3:1-13, 5:17-25; Titus 1:5-16), there are two broad requirements.

The life of the leader—an example

Leaders are to be above reproach and worthy of respect with a demonstrated track-record of leading their own households. They should not be recent converts but must first be tested. There should be no credibility gap between their public and private life, which must be open to scrutiny. Leaders must not be hypocrites, teaching others but not themselves.

In many other places, Paul appeals to the example of his own life as a model of what he taught and as credentials for his leadership (e.g. 1 Cor 11:1; Phil 3:17; 1 Thess 1:6, 2:10).

We are *always* models to our group, whether edifying or not!

The ability of a leader—a teacher

The only ability that is essential for leaders is that they are able to teach. It is the only *skill* Paul requires when choosing elders (see 1 Tim 3 and Titus 1).

Teaching involves two aspects: understanding and communication.

The ability to understand the Bible

As well as having a spirit that is willing to learn, a leader must be able to interpret the Bible with some competence and gain a grasp of its overall message and structure.[1]

The ability to communicate with others

The leader's understanding is useless to the group if he cannot communicate and explain ideas to others. Even though he is teaching through discussion, the leader must be able to guide the group to right conclusions. In some ways this requires more communication skills than in a monologue.

All communication involves both *content* and *rapport*. The content of what the leader says may be superb but if no-one is listening and processing what is said, it is not communication. Rapport is the relational dimension of communication. It is the ability to build bridges to people rather than put up barriers. Whether people understand the meaning of what we say depends to a great extent on how they view us and how they feel towards us. Preconceptions, biases and attitudes all act as filters of communication and distort the message sent and the message received.

We build barriers as leaders and teachers when we project a high status, exhibit a superior attitude, use jargon or even seat ourselves 'above' others.

We build bridges when we learn people's names, enter into the chit-chat over coffee, show genuine interest and are not phoney.

10.5 JOB DESCRIPTION

To be more concrete, here is an outline of the job of a Growth Group leader.

- To lead in Bible study, prayer and evangelism.
- To set the group's goals and agenda and work out its regular program.[2]

---

1   See appendix I for books about understanding the Bible.
2   See training topic 13: *Starting a Growth Group.*

- To be aware of the spiritual state of members and take appropriate action. Are they Christians? In what issues of Christian thinking, behaviour and relationships do they need to grow?[3]
- To get the group working together in love and unity, using their gifts to minister to each other.
- To work in consultation with the church staff/pastors to deal with particular matters beyond the scope of the group.
- To communicate enthusiastically the aims and activities of the wider congregation to which the group belongs.

10.6 LEADERSHIP AS A TEAM

In most Growth Groups, it is best to have the leader working together with an assistant. In larger groups, say more than twelve, other assistants or core members are helpful. These members are 'allies' with you in running the group. They are reliable, energetic people who will always back you up.

Advantages of team leadership

Team leadership has many advantages:
- It provides different perspectives on how the group is operating and on individual group members.
- Division of labour is possible, so that the total weight of responsibility is not carried by one person.
- It is good for the group to see several members serving and thinking of others.
- The leaders learn from each other.
- Assistant leaders can help in the discussion process (see below).

How to make it work

There are a few things to keep in mind in team leadership:

---

3   See training topic 11: *Growing the individuals.*

- One leader should take the overall responsibility of the group.
- Utilize the diversity of each other's gifts, making the most of the differences in personalities, styles, and ministry experiences.
- Plan and prayer together to become of one mind and set clear goals.
- Encourage, don't criticize; if correction is needed, aim to build each other up.
- Be honest and forgiving, not letting disagreements fester into bitterness and anger.

Assisting in a discussion

What role should assistant leaders take when someone else is leading the discussion. It is not their night off! They have a crucial role in making the discussion work. When they are not actually running the discussion, they can observe what is happening in the group and how people are responding. They are like a second pair of eyes and ears for the leader, who is concentrating more on the tasks and content of the discussion. They are free to observe the group processes and can take appropriate actions. This whole process is sometimes called 'group maintenance'.

Here are a couple of tips for assisting in discussion.

Be observant and responsive to the group
- Do they understand the question?
- Was someone interrupted or trying unsuccessfully to get into the discussion?
- Is someone agitated or switched off?

Work with, not against, the leader
- Don't jump in to answer questions yourself.
- Raise a further question or comment that will lead the group down the right path.
- Don't take over; guide unobtrusively.
- Don't argue with the leader.

10.7 YOU CAN CHANGE THE WORLD

That heading sounds like a bad case of megalomania. Not so! God is saving and transforming people through the prayerful teaching of his word. That's what Growth Group leading is all about. Don't be overwhelmed by the responsibility. If you can learn to lead Growth Groups now you will have great opportunities to grow God's people, wherever you are, at every stage of your life.

Here is a true story.

A young engineer with the Department of Main Roads as it was called, moved to a country town in N.S.W. where he found little biblical ministry. So he started a Growth Group (he didn't call it that) with a few other Christians who wanted to study the Bible and pray together. After a while he was moved on but, when he visited the town 10 years later, his Growth Group was still meeting and providing teaching and fellowship for like-minded Christians. His simple strategy has had a permanent influence for Christ in that town. That is the Growth Groups vision.

11

Growing the individuals

We can minister to people in three contexts: large groups, small groups and one-to-one. We choose different contexts for a variety of reasons, including the convenience of gathering people together to say and do the same things. But, ultimately, all ministry is to individuals, proclaiming Christ, "admonishing and teaching everyone with all wisdom, so that we may present everyone perfect in Christ" (Col 1:28).

In leading Growth Groups, our basic concern is not how the group is functioning but the salvation and growth of individuals.

11.1 A KINGDOM FOR LITTLE ONES: MATTHEW 18:1-14

The disciples' timing was immaculate. Jesus had just foreshadowed the arrival of his kingdom through his execution and resurrection (Matt 17:22-23) and all they could think about was their public service grading—who of them would be the greatest in the kingdom of heaven. They had been called to catch people for the kingdom but all they wanted to know was which of them would be the biggest fish in the sea.

Jesus continued his training program with a discourse on 'little ones', complete with visual aid and graphic hyperbole. Seven times he referred to a little child or little one.

Only those who become like children in humility and dependence will enter the kingdom. In God's society, recognizing our weakness brings greatness. Disciples are to welcome other little ones as they have been welcomed. It is a terrible sin to offend one of God's little ones, tripping them up in their discipleship. Even for ourselves, it is better to be maimed than to find ourselves outside the kingdom in hell.

We are not to look down on 'little ones' with the pride of class distinction, since every individual has equal favour before the Father. This Father has the heart of a shepherd who is never happier than in finding the one lost sheep.

It is easier to give general care to the Growth Group than to get involved with individuals. It is hard to welcome some personalities. Some have deep needs and drain us. It takes time and sometimes hardship to draw close. It takes integrity to avoid tripping up others.[1]

11.2 GOD'S AGENDA

Christian ministry operates in two spheres or orbits: God's agenda and the People's agenda. Sometimes these spheres coincide; sometimes they overlap; sometimes they are unrelated.

God's agenda is the salvation and maturity of his people. The People's agenda might vary from a passion for God's agenda to an obsession with personal comfort to any agenda in between. This variation is from holiness to sinfulness.

In our ministry to individuals we need to start with God's agenda. In training topic 1: *The strategy of Growth Groups*, we saw from Colossians that God's desire for his people is that they:

- receive Christ as Lord

    and

- live with Christ as Lord.

---

1 To work through the principles and methods of personal ministry, use the *Six Steps to Encouragement* training course listed in appendix I.

Our aim is to deepen their understanding of God and his salvation in Christ and to provoke a response of faith and obedience in every aspect of life. We are working at both theology (the knowledge of God) and godly practice. Theology without faith is false. Faith without theology is foolish. To know God and ignore him is damnable. To try to please God without listening to him is futile.

In personal ministry we can be quite directive in training our members in theology and godliness. What areas or topics should we cover? There is no definitive syllabus, of course—we just keep teaching the Bible and praying. But there are key topics to have in mind as we talk to our members. This list of key topics is also useful in planning the group teaching.

If we started with Colossians, what key topics would we come up with? Here is a list to which you can add as you study Colossians.

Theology
- the Fatherhood of God
- the grace of God
- the revelation of God in the gospel
- the deity of Christ
- redemption and reconciliation through the cross
- freedom from human religion

Godliness
- prayer
- love and good works
- endurance and patience
- suffering in the ministry of Christ
- dealing with the sinful nature
- forgiveness
- family life
- relating to the world

How would we use such a list? Think of one group member, say, Josephine. Go through the list and ask:
- Does she have clear understanding in these areas?
- Where could I increase her knowledge of God? How could I do it?

- Is she working at godliness in these areas? What areas is she finding difficult? How can I encourage her?

Several benefits come to us as leaders from undertaking this exercise:
- we develop more purposeful prayer
- we may realize that we aren't aware of the spiritual state of our group members
- we learn to listen more actively to our group members.

11.3 THE PEOPLE'S AGENDA

People are not blank sheets of paper. All kinds of influences have made them what they are, with their particular concerns, circumstances and needs. In ministry, we are interacting with the whole person, not just some 'spiritual' part. And God, in his grace, wants to transform the whole of our existence, including the hidden areas of our motivations, fears, temptations and doubts.

The more we understand people, the better we will be able to apply the gospel of grace to their needs. Sometimes we address a 'spiritual' problem head on when the real issue lies just below the surface. For example, in considering the erratic attendance of one of our members, we might want to remind her of passages about denying yourself and taking up your cross daily. However, when the underlying problem is tiredness due to poor health, workaholism, or depression due to missing out on a promotion, we can then address the gospel to these issues. When we minister to the whole person, there is great potential for spiritual growth, because God speaks to us about all aspects of life in this world.

What do we need to know about our flock? What influences have made them what they are? Here are some broad areas to consider:
- family background: ethnicity, geography, social class, stability of parents
- church or religious background
- education
- significant friendships
- interests
- physical: health, sexual needs

- emotions: ambitions, fears, frustrations, self-esteem
- economics: financial needs, pressures and plans
- mind: belief and values

As we listen to our members in the group time and in personal conversation, we will gradually come to know their particular struggles in Christian growth.

11.4 PRAYER FOR GROWTH

Our discussion above gives us lots of fuel for prayer. God's agenda and the People's agenda tell us what to pray for our members. We can pray for their increase in the knowledge of God and his will and for a life worthy of the Lord (Col 1:9-10). We can pray in detail for their needs. We should be thanking God for his grace toward them.

It takes some discipline to pray regularly for our members, so it helps to have a particular plan, such as praying for one member each day or praying weekly with our assistant leaders. Keeping a prayer diary of the requests we are bringing to God may also increase our prayerfulness.

In this course, we are spending a lot of time honing our skills in Bible teaching, but without prayer it is futile. One way to integrate our Bible study preparation and prayer is to pray as you read the passage, with particular group members in mind. We could pray for their understanding and application of God's word in some detail.

Ultimately, the reason we don't pray is unholy pride. We actually think we will change people's lives ourselves, or deep down we think that they are a lost cause and don't believe that any change can occur. Such confidence in our own competence is the enemy of prayer and the antithesis of faithfulness.

11.5 IDEAS FOR PERSONAL MINISTRY

There are limitless possibilities and contexts for one-to-one ministry to our group. Here are some ideas.

Social
- Plan leisure activities such as meals, sports and outings. These build

bridges of trust and understanding and establish more open relationships between group members.

- Use the supper times after the group or at church.

Structured

- Organize 'prayer partners'; meet regularly for prayer with individual members.
- Visit an unbeliever in the group to talk through the gospel and his questions.
- One-to-one Bible reading and prayer, which can take various forms:
  —use follow-up studies for new Christians
  —study the Bible passage scheduled for group discussion
  —read through a book of the Bible over a few weeks
  —use study guides to read a book of the Bible
  —study a Bible topic of particular interest.
- Study a Christian book together.
- Visit members who have been absent or wrestling with some issue.
- Do some ministry together, such as visiting a non-Christian friend.
- Do a ministry training course together.[2]

11.6 ONE-TO-ONE BIBLE READING AND PRAYER

This is a strategic ministry to develop as a lifelong habit. Reading the Bible individually with a Christian or unbeliever is a powerful way of teaching and developing a relationship. It is convenient, even for the most chaotic lifestyles. It is transferable to any context and you don't need to know any more than your friend in order to start. Whatever else you do in Christian ministry, whether you lead Growth Groups or not, look for one spiritually hungry person to meet with for Bible reading and prayer. If you do this for thirty years, thirty growing Christians will benefit from your faithfulness.

---

2   See appendix I for tools and books to assist you in these tasks.

11.7 SOME WARNINGS

Expectations

Growth Group leaders are usually busy people with many responsibilities. You will not be able to do all the personal ministry that is possible. Working with people is open-ended—there is always more to be done. You won't be able to meet with every member every week, or personally visit every absentee. This is where assistant leaders are invaluable, to personalize the ministry without burning out the leader.

We also need some basis for setting the priorities in our personal ministry.

Progress, not problems

Have you ever noticed how people with problems absorb your time and energy? You can feel the energy drain out of you as they enter the room. We all have problems, but some people become problem-centred because of the severity of their needs. One mistake in personal ministry is to be dominated by such people. They are so needy that, in our compassion, we feel guilty if we don't give them all the energy they demand. We end up visiting them again and again, or frequently meeting them at the expense of others.

It may sound harsh at first, but there is a better way. Firstly, if you do meet with problem-centred people, set a different agenda. Instead of starting with their problems again, start with Bible reading and prayer. Then they will start to see how God views their life and problems, and perhaps make some progress in dealing with life under God's word. Secondly, give priority to training others in ministry. Meet with a spiritually hungry, 'problem-free' person who will mature and begin to serve others. You can then give better care to those with problems, because there are more people trained as carers. Investing time in training others in service multiplies the workforce in the group, church and community.

Know your limitations

Some personal problems are well beyond the scope of the Growth Group leader and we may need to refer members to the pastors of the church or to other professionally trained helpers, while providing comfort and security in the group for the person concerned.

Spiritual guru syndrome

We don't want to become spiritual guides for people and make them dependent on us rather than God. Meeting regularly with someone and drawing into close relationship can be highly manipulative. Some have never had such close attention from anyone and they will agree to anything to protect the relationship. To avoid forming such dependency, you may need to set limits of a few weeks or months for regular personal meetings.

The cults have deliberately exploited the power of personal discipleship to control their members and movements. We need to ensure that our personal ministries are characterized by freedom and flexibility. Some people should never be invited to regular personal meetings, because of their insecurities.

11.8 TRAINING LEADERS

One priority in personal ministry is to train new leaders and assistants. This won't always be possible, but we should learn to think in terms of raising up new ministers of God's word. Often as we lead a group it will be evident that one or two of its members should be equipped for leadership. The Growth Group is an ideal setting for such training.[3]

---

3   For more on this see training topic 14: *Selecting, training and shepherding leaders.*

12

The healthy growth group

Our Growth Groups have particular goals: to grow Christians and to further the growth of the gospel. To attain these goals we need to develop a healthy group life, where the relationships in the group are constructive. It is often the *process* of growing a healthy group which contributes to the growth of its members.

Take for example the group where certain members dominate, putting their points aggressively, insisting on their priorities for the group and creating a defensive climate. At one level, they are having a destructive effect on group life. The group isn't healthy and, as its leader, you want to fix it. The downtrodden members need to be more at home and the overbearing characters need to learn a bit of sensitivity. As you work at improving this aspect of group life, both in the group time and one to one, there can be significant Christian growth for everyone. The timid learn to confront and forgive; the tyrants learn to use their power lovingly.

Growth Groups will never be perfectly healthy, because we are not in heaven yet. Every group will have problems. But problems in groups present opportunities for Christian growth. Expect them, welcome them, use them.

One way to consider a healthy Growth Group is to look at what the Bible says about Christian relationships, as we have been doing in our study of Colossians. Another method is to use a diagnostic tool, such as the one below.

12.1 A DIAGNOSTIC TOOL: WHAT ARE THE INDICATORS OF A HEALTHY GROWTH GROUP?

This list of indicators provides a diagnostic tool to use like a stethoscope to evaluate the health of your Growth Group.[1]

Each of the characteristics mentioned is fundamental to Christian relationships which are shaped by God's generosity and openness in giving his Son. We involve others in our Growth Group because God has welcomed us. We listen to others' contribution because God listens to us and treats us with dignity. We can be open with each other because God sees all that we are and yet calls us his children.

Ownership: each member belongs to the group

In a healthy group, members will feel a sense of 'ownership' about the group.

Symptoms of a healthy group:

- Each member is committed to the group goals.
- Each member has concern for the progress of the group.
- Each member fulfils a particular role in the group.
- They talk about 'our' group, not 'their' group or the leader's group.
- High attendance rates.
- Willingness to stay after the formal meeting.

Diagnostic questions:

- Do some people seem to be part of an 'in' group? Are others on the 'outside'?
- Are there sub-groups where two or three members consistently agree with or relate to each other or, conversely, oppose each other?
- What are the attendance patterns?

---

1 Some of this material has been adapted from *Group Leadership* produced by the Health Promotion Unit, Program Development Branch, NSW Department of Health.

Participation: high levels of involvement in discussion

In a discussion, someone gets the ball rolling—usually, the leader. Initially, the members interact with the leader, with different members responding in turn. It's like tennis with a different opponent for each shot.

The leader's aim is to make discussion more like volleyball than tennis, with a complex, unpredictable series of interactions between all members. The leader is still guiding the discussion, but at times fades into the background.[2]

Symptoms of a healthy group:

- Everyone participating at the level they desire.
- Members communicating effectively, their intended meaning being understood.
- No-one dominating the air-time.
- Avoidance of long two-way conversations with others just observing.
- Absence of unwritten rules or patterns that inhibit communication (e.g. "We shouldn't disagree with others, especially the leader"; "Interrupt others if you want to get into the discussion"; "Only smart, well thought-out comments are accepted here").

Diagnostic questions:

- Who are high and low frequency contributors?
- Are there shifts in participation, such as high contributors going quiet? Is there anything that has happened in the group that could explain this?
- How are the quiet people treated? How is their silence interpreted? Consent? Disagreement? Disinterest? Anxiety?
- Who talks to whom? Why?
- Do some members move in and out of the discussion, maybe leaning forward and back in their chairs? At what points in the discussion do they do this?
- Which members influence others? Who can get others to listen to them?
- Which members have little influence?
- Is there any rivalry in the group? A struggle for power?

---

2   See training topic 5: *Leading a Bible study.*

Openness: honesty in self-disclosure

Openness is important in Christian groups. To be honest with God and each other is a prerequisite for growth in Christ. If we are hiding our fears and doubts we cannot receive the comfort of the gospel. If we are covering our sins, we cannot receive the rebuke and forgiveness of the gospel. If we are reserved about our joys and victories, we deny the reality of the gospel.

Openness in the group ultimately stems from a confidence in being acceptable to God through Christ. We are laid bare before a holy God who welcomes us in Christ—we can cope with the vulnerability of being slightly exposed in the group.

Symptoms of a healthy group:
- Emotions are expressed in the group.
- Others are helped to express emotions.
- The group is not frozen when deep emotions are expressed.
- Honest struggle with applications from Bible study.
- Honesty in prayer.
- Acceptance of different personalities.
- Acceptance of criticism without withdrawal, resentment or anger.

Diagnostic questions:
- Are there any taboo topics?
- Are only positive feelings expressed?
- Are members overly nice and polite to each other?
- In what manner are ideas rejected?
- How do members react when their ideas are not accepted?
- What feelings do you observe in group members: anger, irritation, warmth, affection, excitement, boredom, defensiveness, competitiveness?
- What are the signs of these emotions: tone of voice, facial expressions, gestures?
- Do group members try to block the expression of negative feelings? How is this done?

Service: each member using their gifts

The New Testament stresses the variety of gifts and ministries to be exercised by Christians (1 Cor 12, 14; Rom 12; Eph 4; 1 Pet 4). This variety originates from God, who bestows all good gifts on his creatures. These passages illustrate the diversity of gifts and are not meant to be a definitive catalogue. It is often difficult to define exactly the nature of a particular gift listed in these passages because they are not described, only listed.

Gifts are given by God for the growth and unity of his people, and are to be used in love, not in envy and rivalry. There is no limit to the gifts and abilities of God's people. Whatever anyone can contribute to the common good of believers is a gift from God and is to be used faithfully. We shouldn't categorize gifts as 'spiritual' or 'natural', because *all* our abilities come from God, be they cooking, listening to others or leading in prayer. And the gifts of God can be nurtured by training and practice.

There is a wide variety of gifts that can be exercised in a Growth Group: teaching, social organizing, hospitality, music, letter writing, contacting absentees, and so on. Some are concrete tasks, while others are more relational and informal but important for the quality of the group time.

Symptoms of a healthy group:
- Tasks are shared by members according to their gifts.
- It is recognized that members will not perform every task.
- The leader is aware of the abilities of the group.
- Members feel they belong and have particular roles to fulfil.
- Members are experimenting to see if they can be useful to the group in new ways.
- The leader is honestly guiding members about their gifts, encouraging them in areas of strength and pointing out weaker areas.

Diagnostic questions:
- Who is performing what formal tasks?
- What roles are being adopted informally?
  Constructive: encourager, peacemaker, empathizer, initiator, summarizer, humorist, devil's advocate.

Destructive: clown, sympathy seeker, avoider, sidetracker, monopolizer, expert.[3]

Achievement: the group goals are being achieved

A healthy group will make progress towards its set goals and see some of these goals attained. Some achievements may be difficult to measure, such as changes in people's beliefs. However, most changes will be expressed in one way or another.

Symptoms of a healthy group:
- Members are conscious of their own growth.
- The focus on tasks doesn't weaken relational aspects of the group.
- There is a balance of Bible study, prayer and evangelism.

Diagnostic questions:
- What are members praying about?
- Are group members preparing for Bible study?
- Is there a sense of struggling with obedience to God?
- Is there a concern for evangelism?

12.2 CAUSES OF AN UNHEALTHY GROUP

We have seen above the characteristics of a healthy group, providing its leader with a diagnostic tool with which to assess the state of the group. But what factors make a group unhealthy? If we can work out what is causing the group to function in an unhealthy way, we can take some remedial steps.

The following are some possible causes of ill-health, springing from the individual, the interaction between members, the leaders and from the group context itself.

The individual

Sometimes, the cause of an unhealthy group is focused on an individual. Jane

---

3   See also training topic 7: *The games people play.*

comes to the group, sits in a corner and says very little except to jump down someone's throat when she disagrees on a minor issue. This is not typical for Jane. As we enquire, we find it is nothing to do with the functioning of the group. She lost her job that day. The personalities, mood and circumstances of individuals have a huge bearing on the functioning of the group.

The members

Lack of trust and acceptance

In the early stages of a group, members are often anxious about how they will be treated. They can be afraid of failing, looking stupid and being rejected, or just be uncertain of what is expected of them. Often, the group copes with this lack of trust by preoccupying itself with tasks. Members will use a variety of tactics to avoid threatening topics: rushing through material rather than pursuing it in-depth; fussing over rules and procedures; being overly polite.

As trust develops, members will take more risks, offering ideas and opinions and revealing more of their true selves behind the public image.

How to build trust:
- Teach the gospel of confession and forgiveness (read 1 John 1).
- The leader's model will affect the group—remember names; encourage all contributors.
- Discriminate between the value and truthfulness of contributions. Members need to know they can offer any idea, but they will respect the leader and group which makes sincere judgments about its truth or value. People want to know where they stand with each other.
- Appropriate self-disclosure by the leader. Too much too soon will scare people off.
- Establish the ground rule of confidentiality. This will encourage security in self-disclosure.
- Encourage friendships beyond the group time.
- Informality in the group over meals, outings, etc.
- In summary: by proving to be worthy of that trust.

Unresolved conflict

Conflict is a normal part of Growth Groups because it is a normal part of relating in this world. Not only should we expect conflict, we should welcome it. It provides a window of opportunity for the growth of individuals and the group. In resolving conflict, godly attitudes and behaviour are encouraged and there is often a need to repent from sin.

There are different sources of conflict:
- personality clashes
- differing goals and expectations
- differing beliefs and values
- power struggles.

People make various responses to conflict and have different ways of handling it:
- denial
- fight to win
- avoid it
- compromise
- capitulate.

What should Christians do in conflict situations?
- Be willing to face them honestly; it is happening.
- Look to our own attitudes and sins that may be contributing to the conflict.
- Admit our anger or frustrations.
- Confront others with the problems they are causing.
- Be generous with forgiveness and patience.
- Look for mutually beneficial solutions.
- Sometimes back down.

The leader

Failure to establish ground rules for group life

Every society has rules of behaviour or laws which are designed to promote the good of the individual and the society as a whole. In little societies like our

Growth Groups, certain patterns of behaviour will be beneficial to achieving the aims of the group. Others will be a hindrance.

Lots of these patterns have been touched on already: listening to all contributions; not interrupting each other; the freedom to disagree with each other; keeping confidences shared in the group; the freedom to ask questions. However, there ought not be too many conscious rules, as this will suffocate the group.

These ground rules are set in two ways:

- Implicitly by the models set by the leader and others.
- Explicitly by discussion and agreement. The Bible itself will shape godly patterns of how others are to be treated.

The ground rules can be enforced in two ways:

- By group pressure: the majority agree that a particular pattern is right and the members find it impossible to resist.
- By the admonition of the leader or other member, privately or in the group.

Imbalance between task and relationship

Some groups are so focused on the job at hand that the members become alienated from each other. In other groups, so much time is spent 'holding each other's hands' that nothing gets done.

We need to stick to our agenda of Bible study, prayer, serving each other and reaching out. If we don't, there will be no growth. But if the group or particular members are unhappy, it is impossible to work through a Bible study or prayer time in a way that benefits the whole group.

Do we always have to complete our planned program for the night? Sometimes, the agenda has to be set aside to deal with issues affecting the group. It may be a matter external to the group, such as a member in grief over a personal tragedy. Or it may be internal to the group, such as hostility between two members.

At other times, the maintenance of relationships is simultaneous with the task.

How can we ensure the relationships are maintained?

- Accept people's contributions.

- Draw others into the discussion.
- Notice that a member wants to say something.
- Admit mistakes and seek forgiveness.
- Clarify differences and reconcile disagreements.
- Be conscious of which members are focused on the task and which members are sensitive to relationships.

The group
The physical environment
Seating arrangements
Seating has a powerful effect on group dynamics. There needs to be eye contact between all members, with all seated at roughly the same level. The seating should not be focused around the leaders. Leaders should sit where they can see people as they arrive. Seats need to be comfortable to avoid distraction: sitting on the floor creates a lethargic mood; sitting around a table creates a study environment.

The position of certain personalities in the group will alter dynamics. A lot of it has to do with eye contact which, in turn, affects participation. Sit dominant members near the leader to minimize eye contact with them. Quieter members should sit opposite the leader to increase eye contact. Quieter members might feel overawed if sitting between two 'bigger' people, either in size or personality.

Acoustics
Eliminate background noise and distractions. Choose a location where all can hear each other without straining. The telephone can be a problem if you are meeting in a busy home.

Lighting
Lighting affects the mood of a group. Soft lighting is more intimate, but difficult for reading. Bright light behind members makes them hard to see and draws them out of the discussion.

Ventilation
Stuffy rooms make for sleepy discussions. The air temperature ought to be comfortable: neither too hot nor too cold.

Events

Things that happen in the group can have a long term effect on its functioning. These may be recent or quite distant events. Suppose one or two members at the first meeting of the group spoke openly about some highly emotive personal issues. The group may remain reserved, not wanting to cope with further outpourings. Then again, it might become normal for people to be emotionally charged when they speak about personal issues.

Structure

There will be a pattern or network of relationships in a group. There may be sub-groups, cliques or power structures, such as a minority group which repeatedly hijacks the discussion. These will all have an effect on the group. Quiet groups may be caused by cliques who do not know or relate to the others.

The leader can set up new structures by varying the format of the discussion: use prayer partners, buzz groups for short discussions, syndicates for research and reporting, debating teams, role plays.

Content

The content or topic of discussion may suppress the group for a variety of reasons. It may be too difficult, beyond their knowledge or experience, too easy and obvious, too intimidating or too repetitive.

Atmosphere or mood

The overall temper of your group will effect things like participation levels. A group might be energetic, sluggish, congenial, argumentative, hardworking or playful.

12.3 DIAGNOSING A SICK GROWTH GROUP

There are three stages in the diagnosis of a group:

1. Make accurate observations

The diagnostic tool above (12.1) provides a 'stethoscope' for assessing the health of a group. You need to get into the habit of using this stethoscope to diagnose the condition of your group. Use it to make accurate observations of what is happening. Regularly ask yourself and your assistant leaders the diagnostic questions.

Take care when interpreting observations. The same event can have several possible interpretations. For example, two members conducting a private conversation during the discussion could mean they are bored, stimulated, angry or in love!

2. Determine the cause(s) of ill health

Once some unhealthy aspect of group life has been observed, the causes need to be analyzed so that a remedy can be applied. Many common causes of ill health have been canvassed above (12.2). Usually, there is not one isolated cause of ill health, so it is important to consider all possible factors. It always helps to check your diagnosis with your assistant leaders.

3. Apply the remedy

Having made observations of unhealthy aspects of group life and diagnosed probable causes, the final step is to work out what action should be taken to remedy the situation. In some cases, no action is best, either because the problem will correct itself as the group grows in Christ, or because tackling the problem would distract the group from its more central aims of growth. You and the group might decide to live with the problem.

Possible remedies have been suggested above, focusing on the individual, the members, the leader and the group. Some remedies are direct, others more subtle.

12.4 A CASE STUDY

This case study illustrates how to use the diagnostic tool to assess the health of a Growth Group and how to determine the causes of ill-health.

Consider a group of 12 members from the same church, who meet once a week on a Wednesday evening. Few of the members knew each other before joining the group. Their ages range from 19 to 40, all singles.

1. Observations

Using the diagnostic tool, we look carefully at the behaviour of the group.

The group is quiet and not participating well in discussions. This pattern has continued for several weeks, not just in the early stage. They are overly polite and 'nice' to each other, never expressing negative feelings about anything. One member of the group dominates the air time. The group tends to rush through material rather than pursuing in-depth discussion.

2. Possible causes of ill health

Here we consider the possible causes of an unhealthy group mentioned at 12.2.

THE INDIVIDUALS
Three group members are quiet personalities. They seem comfortable; they are just quiet.

THE MEMBERS
Trust and acceptance?
There are low levels of trust evidenced by an avoidance of expressing negative feelings and a lack of in-depth discussion.

Unresolved conflict?
No evidence.

THE LEADER
Failure to establish ground rules for group life?
No, this was done.

Imbalance between task and relationship?
Yes, this is a problem, evidenced by rushing through discussion material.

THE GROUP
The physical environment
The seating at different heights is reducing eye contact.

Events

One member poured out a personal problem on the first night which the group didn't know how to handle. This memory could be an inhibiting factor.

Structure

The group seems to be intimidated by its size.

Content

Not a particular problem, as these studies have worked well in other groups.

Atmosphere or mood

There aren't many outgoing personalities in the group.

3. Apply the remedy

Some causes have no obvious remedy. The three quiet personalities may warm up as time goes on, but they are what they are and need to be accepted. Not everyone is outgoing, nor would we want everyone to be. The personality of group members must become part of the way the group operates.

Other causes suggest their own remedies. A friendship-building activity, like a holiday or helping a member build a garage, should create trust—as long as the garage stays up. Acquiring more chairs would fix the seating problem. You could review the ground rule of the freedom to express strong feelings and discuss the event which occurred on the first night. Breaking the group into smaller units of three or four for some exercises, and having these groups report back to the big group, may free up discussion.

Starting a growth group

Starting a growth group is exciting because it is creative. You are creating something new. An assortment of individuals wanders into your lounge room on the first night, reserved, tentative, polite, testing the waters to see if they like it. A few weeks or months down the track, the individuals have become a group. They study together, laugh and cry with each other, pray, open up to each other, notice when someone is missing.

What does it take to form a Growth Group? Here are some guidelines.

13.1 SET AND ARTICULATE A CLEAR OVERALL PURPOSE FOR THE GROUP

In training topic 1: *The strategy of Growth Groups*, we defined two overall goals for Growth Groups.

1. Christian growth

Through Growth Groups we want our group members to grow in Christ, which means they will:

*   receive Christ as Lord
    and
*   live with Christ as Lord.

2. Gospel growth

Through Growth Groups we want the gospel to grow and bear fruit.

These goals need to be discussed and agreed upon as the group is formed. Without common goals there will be no cohesion in the group.

13.2 SET THE AGENDA EARLY

As we saw in training topic 2: *Growth Group basics*, there are some basic activities for Christians to mature in Christ and for the growth of the gospel.

Prayer

In Growth Groups we pray for ourselves and others through group prayer and in prayer partners.

Hearing God's word

In Growth Groups we hear God's word through Christ-centred Bible study.

Proclaiming God's word

In Growth Groups we proclaim Christ personally and through group activities.

The agenda of the group can be set in two ways:

- The leader explains it to the group.
- The leader engages the group in the activities mentioned above.

The latter is the more powerful approach. Right from the start, the group should engage in Bible study, prayer and concern for outsiders, and so demonstrate what the group will be doing together.

13.3 BE AWARE OF A VARIETY OF EXPECTATIONS

We need a clear purpose in our minds for the group so that we can explain to the group why we are meeting and give it firm direction. However, people come to groups with different expectations. Some want deeper friendships or just to be accepted; others are more concerned about the content and learning from discussion; still others will focus more on their role and influence over others.

We need to recognize the legitimacy of each person's needs and reasons for joining. But if the leader doesn't set a clear exciting vision for the group, these competing interests will create tensions. And when members' expectations are not fulfilled, there is a loss of motivation and absenteeism sets in.

In the end, needs such as friendship will be met through achieving our goals of Christian growth and gospel growth. If there is no love for each other within the group, we obviously still have some distance to travel to reach our goals.

Setting out the purpose of a Growth Group begins way back at the 'recruiting' stage, when we invite members to join the group on the basis of our goals of growth in Christ.

13.4 BE UP-FRONT ABOUT THE COMMITMENT REQUIRED

We have all been in groups with fringe members who are not really committed to the group. Their attendance is patchy; they turn up late; they grumble about the group and only participate if the mood strikes them. They have a devastating effect on the morale of the leader and group.

There are many facets of group life that affect commitment, such as not having a role, felt needs not being met, the dominance of the leader, a lack of interest in individuals or a spiritual problem. These are dealt with in training topic 12: *The healthy Growth Group*.

But the way the group is formed is crucial. There are two possible approaches:

- **Gather the group, then spell out the commitments**
  This usually results in low levels of commitment. The leader becomes apologetic and powerless, paralyzed for fear of someone deciding to leave because their expectations are not being met.

- **Spell out the commitments as members are recruited**
  People respond well to positive leadership and knowing what they are getting into. Commitments would include areas such as: attendance, punctuality, preparation, participation and willingness to contribute to the evangelistic effort of the group. This is the preferred approach.

There will always be some absenteeism, even in the most committed groups. As group leader, always give yourself to the ones who have come and don't fret or become distracted by the non-attenders. It is not right that those who have turned up should be disadvantaged because of the leader's emotional distraction.

13.5 PLAN THE LOGISTICS

Who to invite

Different groups will work with different types of members, depending upon the group's purpose. For evangelistic purposes, it is useful to bring together people from a common 'affinity group'. Affinity groups are people who naturally associate together because of factors such as age, common interests, work, locality or place in society.[1]

When to hold the group and how often

Weekly meetings work best for most people because they organize most of life on a weekly basis. The time of a weekly meeting needs to be lifestyle-friendly, suiting your particular target group.

Set a termination point

It is best to run groups that have a finite life span rather than being of indefinite duration. If you set a termination or review point after a year, for example, this provides a way out for leaders and members, if there is a need for such a change.[2]

---

1   See training topic 9: *Gospel growth through Growth Groups* for more on this approach to forming a group.
2   More on this in training topic 15: *Developing the Growth Group program*.

How many to include

The size of the group should allow for the active participation of all members. This usually means that 6-12 members will be ideal. With less than six, the group is too intense, with all members having to participate all the time. In small groups, any absenteeism tends to lower morale severely. With more than twelve, it becomes too easy for members to hide or be passive, and attendance drops off because there is a sense of not being missed among the many other members.

Where to meet

Considerations are: comfortable seating with everyone at the same level, ventilation, heating, lighting, not being too cramped for space and having an accessible location.

13.6 UNDERSTAND THE STAGES OF GROUP LIFE[3]

Groups tend to go through certain phases. Understanding this will help the leader to deal with unrealistic expectations and disappointments, particularly when a group is getting under way. The duration of each phase will vary from group to group.

The tentative stage

What are group members thinking and feeling when they first come to a group?

I feel awkward here ... Can I trust these people if I talk about myself? ... I'll let the leader run the show ... Who is in control here? ... Do I fit? ... How will I benefit? ... What influence will I have? ... Do I like these people? ... Will I stay?

Most people make a tentative commitment to the group and test the waters.

---

3   Some of this material has been adapted from *Getting Together* by Em Griffin (IVP, Downers Grove, 1982).

The leader's role in this stage is to:
- Give clear directive leadership to create a sense of purpose and security.
- Set clear goals.
- Establish ground rules for how the group will function and members' responsibilities.
- Show interest in each member.

The settled stage

This is the 'healthy group' stage.[4] The group is experiencing:
- Ownership: each member belongs to the group
- Participation: high levels of involvement in discussion
- Openness: honesty in self-disclosure
- Service: each member using his or her gifts
- Achievement: the group goals are being achieved

The leader's role and strategy to reach and maintain this settled stage is to:
- Create shared experiences which will build a healthy group. Anything from wearing a uniform to picking a street fight with some local hoods (just kidding!) will create a sense that "we are the group that did this thing together". The shared memories contribute to group identity. More likely strategies include: meals, outings, weekends away, games, singing, evangelism.
- Delegate and share responsibilities.
- Review the goals and commitments to the group, helping members to see both individual and group progress, as well as what is yet to be achieved.

The complacent stage

This is a dangerous stage. Its symptoms include boredom as routine sets in, a lower commitment to the group and uncertainty about the future.

The leader's role and strategy to escape this stage is to:

---

4   See training topic 12: *The healthy Growth Group.*

- Be more directive as in the earlier stages of group life.
- Be enthusiastic, encouraging perseverance.
- Set new aims.
- Spawn a daughter group.[5]
- Possibly bring the group to an end.

The termination stage

This subject is dealt with in training topic 15: *Developing the Growth Group program.*

13.7 THE FIRST MEETING

The agenda of the first meeting flows from what we have discussed above:
- Discuss the purpose and activities of the group.
- Review the agreed commitments.
- Read the Bible and pray to establish this as the central activity of the group. A short, easy study will work best in promoting participation and removing initial anxieties.
- Have some fun (food, ice-breaker activities).

The most important goal of the first meeting is universal participation: everyone must say something in the group. It doesn't matter how trivial the contribution, as long as everyone opens their mouths. The longer a person delays contributing to the group, the harder it gets.

---

5 See training topic 15: *Developing the Growth Group program.*

Selecting, training and shepherding leaders

14.1 WHY WE SHOULD

The quality of a group is determined by the quality of its leaders. The careful selection, training and supervision of leaders takes time and effort but pays great dividends. To develop a Growth Groups program, someone has to give priority to raising up and encouraging leaders. In most churches, this person needs to be the pastor.

There are enormous advantages to the pastor selecting and training the leaders. He should not see this work as a distraction but rather as the heart and soul of his work. By doing the selection and training himself, he ensures high 'quality control' (to borrow a commercial term) of the Growth Groups. He will know the strengths and weaknesses of each leader. He draws into personal relationship with each leader during the training process and they catch his vision for Christ and the church. In some cases, the pastor may want to delegate the training; for example, a woman on his staff might train women in teaching and leadership, though this need not always be the case.

Pastors need to grasp the strategy of equipping godly, skilful teachers within the congregation. A pastor working on his own may be able to build up a congregation of 100 or even 150. Beyond that, it is difficult to have enough contact with the members for effective personal ministry. A team of Growth Group leaders will add depth and quality to the work and facilitate expansion.

Many pastors, not one

All through the New Testament, we see a pattern of having many leaders serving the one congregation. In some situations, we see one minister with overall responsibility. For example, Paul took leadership of the young congregations born through the gospel he preached (Acts 20:31). He also appointed his delegates, Timothy and Titus to lead churches.

We can think of these leaders as 'missionaries', because they have come from outside the congregation to preach and plant the new church. These 'missionary' leaders were financially supported by the churches so that they could give themselves without distraction to the work (1 Cor 9:3-12; 2 Cor 11:7-12; Phil 4:14-19). Once the New Testament churches were established, local elders were appointed from within the church.

We see also in the New Testament the pattern of 'tent-making', where Paul supported himself by paid employment, for the sake of ministry (Acts 18:1-4; 1 Cor 9:12-18; 1 Thess 2:6-9).

Sometimes, New Testament teachers have a title, such as 'overseer', 'elder' or 'leader' (Acts 20:25-31; 1 Tim 3:1-7, 5:17-20; Titus 1:5-9; Heb 13:7). In other places, they are given no title but are expected to teach (Rom 15:14; Eph 4:15; Col 3:15-17; 2 Tim 2:1-2; Titus 2:1-5; 1 Pet 4:10-11). Some teachers were supported financially to direct the church through their teaching ministry (1 Tim 5:17-18).

It would be quite appropriate in New Testament terms to call Growth Group leaders 'elders' or 'pastors'.

A church should have many pastors or elders, not one. The chief pastor, who is usually full-time and paid, needs a team of lay pastors to do the work properly. They will be people who work in other paid jobs, 'tent-making' in order to do ministry without draining the financial resources of the congregation.

14.2 WHY WE DON'T

The paid minister of a church is pulled in a multitude of directions. Everyone thinks they own the minister. There is a constant tension between his priorities and goals, and the demands being placed upon him. Training for leadership seems like just one more good thing to do. Leaders of Growth Groups can feel the same sort of tensions, if not to the same degree.

Below are some of the tensions that can be felt in relation to training leaders. In most cases, they are as relevant to a Growth Group leader as they are to the paid minister of a church.

The immediate versus long-term

There is enough to do just to keep the program running, with preaching, visitation, 'hatch, match and despatch', committees and weekly crises to resolve. Training lay leaders is hard to fit in.

But choosing not to do it is *short-term thinking*. If training is a priority, the long-term result will be more and better workers. Instead of the minister doing all the people-work, there will be others on the team, and much of the spiritual growth will take place in the small groups.

Using people versus developing people

Ministers tend to be need-driven rather than resource-driven. In managing the church program, personnel needs can be urgent and can dominate our horizon. People are recruited to plug the gaps in the leadership of the Sunday School, the youth group, the church committee and Bible study groups. Whatever else happens, there is a feeling that the status quo must be maintained and all of the current programs kept running. Every year there is the scramble for workers and a series of awkward conversations with people who may not wish to lead but just can't say no.

If we turn the process around, looking at our resources instead of needs, we have a better chance of providing a well-trained, enthusiastic leadership. Imagine if a minister were to hypothetically scrap all the church's current programs, sit down with the church membership roll and ask himself the following questions about each member:

- What do they really want to do?
- What are their gifts?
- What would be their best contribution to the ministry?
- What nurture, training and encouragement do they need?

This approach might not result in all the old programs continuing, but imagine how the members would feel: loved, motivated, relieved, free. In taking this approach, we have moved from *using* people to *developing* people.

Instead of determining the church program by precedent and then trying to fill the personnel needs, this approach will see new ministries evolve around members who are equipped, confident and gifted in their particular work. You may have no-one to run the youth work in your church, but there may be a Vietnamese couple who would love to reach their compatriots and need to be equipped for this. You may struggle to find an organizer of the men's fellowship, but there may be a married couple who would love to start a Growth Group in their area and need some training. The work amongst men may flounder until a suitable leader is trained, but the work amongst couples will surge ahead. It is better that these new ministries be done than that old ones continue without appropriate leadership.

If we equip God's people, we will see ministry develop around them. God works through people, not our programs.

Physical versus human resources

Sometimes we are so preoccupied with the physical resources of the church that the development of people is forfeited. It takes enormous energy to set the budget, raise the funds, worry about shortfalls, renovate and expand buildings. If the pastor can delegate at least some of these concerns, he will have more energy for the training of leadership.

14.3 WHOM TO SELECT

We looked at several criteria for selecting leaders in training topic 10: *Leading for growth*. There is something of an art to choosing leaders. It is a matter of developing a nose for it—learning to make useful observations. What should we look for as we work side-by-side with our group members?

- **Who is leading others?**
  One thing leaders need is followers. Look for those who already have a healthy influence over others, leading them informally.

- **Who is already encouraging others in Christian growth?**
  Look for those who take up ministry opportunities without being asked. They will have a servant heart and a love for others, and are not seeking prestige in being an appointed leader.

- **Who is wrestling with the Bible and theology?**
  Look for people who are often asking you good questions and reading books you recommend, as well as the Bible. These people will make good teachers. Do they help others in the group to understand the Bible?

- **Who is sorting out issues of godliness?**
  Those who are hard-hearted and unrepentant should not lead. Leaders should have a blameless reputation within the group, the congregation and the world.

14.4 HOW TO TRAIN LEADERS

Ministry is not learnt in the classroom, hearing lectures on how to lead a group. Like all skills, leadership is learnt on the job. It is a process of receiving instruction, observing good models, having a go at the task, getting feedback, having another go and repeating the process.

Ministry is caught not taught. Ministry is much more than skills. It arises out of who we are before God, what we understand of him, how we have responded to his gospel, how we view and treat other people, and our priorities and passions. We bring to ministry all that we are: our beliefs, values, emotions, experiences and behaviour.

The best leadership training is, therefore, the **apprenticeship model**, where the trainer runs a Growth Group with trainees under his wing. It is more labour intensive than running a 10-week course for 100 people. But it imparts a whole way of living and thinking, rather than merely training technicians. Your aim in leadership training is to reproduce yourself. That may seem off-putting, but it is how you multiply your ministry. It's not that you reproduce clones who copy your personality and mannerisms. Rather, you grow leaders who have the knowledge, skills and heart for the job. And you have seen them in action, so you know their strengths and weaknesses.

This training course is based on the apprenticeship model, because there are opportunities to practise skills and give feedback, and the trainer can impart his vision and heart for the work.

14.5 SHEPHERDING LEADERS

It is tempting to neglect leaders once they have been trained and are under way. Don't do this! In some ways, they need more, not less, input at this point, especially when they are new in the job.

Leaders need in-service training and encouragement. This can be provided through regular meetings with a pastor, talking and praying about their own lives as well as those in their group. Progress and problems in the group can be raised. Particular personal concerns for group members can be considered.

Developing the growth group program

15.1 LONG TERM STRATEGY

Paul had a big vision for the growth of Christians and the growth of the gospel. Nothing less than perfection in Christ was his aim for everyone: "We proclaim him, admonishing and teaching everyone with all wisdom, so that we may present everyone perfect in Christ" (Col 1:28). Paul knew that the gospel was to be proclaimed throughout the world: "All over the world this gospel is bearing fruit and growing" (Col 1:6).

Gathering Christians together for Bible study, prayer and evangelism is central to this vision of reaching everyone with the gospel of Christ. We want to see millions of Growth Groups around the world. Some will be associated with local churches; some with schools and universities; others with the military or the business world. We want to see them in every area of society. For some, the Growth Group will be their only church, especially in areas where the gospel is breaking new ground or where there is persecution and restrictions on the congregating of believers.

15.2 WHERE TO START

There are two general scenarios in which you might find yourself: firstly, one where there are no Growth Groups; secondly, where there is an existing program of small groups that needs development.

No groups

You may be in a church with no Growth Groups, or have moved to a new area where there is nothing like this. You may want to get something started at work, in a neighbourhood, at a school or a tertiary institution.

The key is to *start small*. Gather together those who will be committed to the group rather than trying to accommodate everyone. The half-hearted will bleed the group dry. If you start small and it works, others will see the effects and want to join.

In a church situation, the pastor may or may not support you. He might be paranoid about little groups meeting if he isn't kept informed about what's going on. Always seek the pastor's support and keep him informed. If the group grows in commitment to the central congregation and the pastor, he won't complain and will probably want to see more groups formed.

Existing program

In many churches there will be a small group program operating. Some common problems develop in these programs:

- A diversity of groups exists, with confused aims and lack of direction. The groups have sprung up at different times, as someone acted on an idea, without any overall strategy.
- Some groups have met for many years and are bored to death.
- Group leaders are very independent and resist being part of a coordinated strategy which the pastor wants to implement.
- Only a minority of church members are in groups.

Again, the best approach is to start small. You may be the pastor or small groups coordinator and want to develop an integrated ministry of Growth Groups for all members. If you scrap everything that's already happening and insist on everyone joining your new program of groups, there will be a lot of resistance and little outcome.

Here is a general model of how to develop the program:

Year 1   1 group
Start one group with keen members
Identify four potential leaders and train them in leadership

Year 2   3 groups
Start two new groups with the leaders you have trained
Add new members to the first group
Identify and train eight new leaders

Year 3   7 groups
Start four new groups with the new leaders
Add new members to the first three groups
Identify and train sixteen new leaders

Year 4   15 groups
Keep going!

With this model, you produce high quality leaders whose ministry will ensure that others become enthusiastic about joining groups. You won't need to use 'high-pressure selling' to find people to join these groups, because others will see Christians growing before their eyes.

15.3 WHEN TO END A GROWTH GROUP

Should we ever close down a group? Definitely, yes!

Many groups get to a stage where they just meet because they have always met. They are very comfortable with each other, the roles are very well defined and they are bored. There is no sense of making it work any more—it just happens every week. There is no struggling together over the Scriptures or prayer or reaching others. It has all become too predictable. Without struggle it is dead.

But tensions will run high if you just tell the group they are no longer going to meet. Some creative leadership is required. In a tired group, it may be that new life will be breathed into it by setting out a new challenge. Ask them to spawn a new group with their experienced leaders and add new members to the existing group. Or combine with another group to achieve a new purpose.

In some groups, the tensions within the group become so high and unresolvable that it is better to start again with a new membership than burn out the leader and the group.

Whatever the case, it still takes guts to shoot a dead horse. Small group pastors should also be small group terminators.

How to end it

It is demoralizing for everyone concerned to let a group slowly die, with numbers gradually dropping until the group has absolutely no pulse. It is much better to end with a bang rather than a whimper. Good things can be accomplished at a final meeting.

- Set the final date early enough so that all can attend.
- Review the highlights of the group and the more memorable incidents.
- Give some perspective on how the group has moved through different stages.
- Discuss the growth seen in the group and individuals, with members offering their observations.
- Pray and give thanks for the growth God has given. This should be the focus of this final time together, since the purpose of the group was Christian growth.
- Avoid negative feedback at this stage. It is not an encouraging way to end. If some start making negative comments about the group, it can easily snowball into a gripe session, with every little problem being reviewed. There are two ways to avoid this: firstly, the leader can acknowledge problems that occurred and how they were handled; secondly, ask the review questions in a positive mode: "What growth in our lives has God given this year?"
- Acknowledge the loss that members will experience as the group concludes and suggest ways to compensate for this. For some, the emotional support from the group has been significant. For others, they will need to find new contexts for Christian growth. Encourage them into other Growth Groups and into one-to-one fellowship.

15.4 FIXED TERM GROUPS

Another approach is to have all groups in a church run on a one or two year cycle. This circumvents the awkward problem of terminating groups. At the end of the term, everyone is given the opportunity to change groups. This can be refreshing for leaders and members. Difficult relationships in groups can be diffused by changing groups. There is no awkwardness about this occurring, because lots of members are doing the shuffle.

Fixed-term groups also prevent long-term cliques developing.

Of course if members and leaders want to stay together longer, they can. But the fixed-term approach makes it easier for new members to join, because each year there is a starting point for groups. They don't have to join a group that has met for years and so struggle to fit in.

A typical program:

January, yr 1:	Invite members to join one of ten groups
November, yr 1:	All groups close down for holiday period
January, yr 2:	Invite members to join one of fourteen groups

15.5 OPEN OR CLOSED GROUPS?

Do we open up our groups to new members at any time or should the membership of a Growth Group by and large be closed after the group has commenced meeting?

Closed membership seems to be a contradiction of our goals, given our ethos of Growth Groups as expansive and outward looking. There is no justification for introspective groups focused on their own existence and comfort. Growth Groups are never an end in themselves. However, if we are always adding new members, the group never develops cohesion and intimacy at its meetings. It is always a group of strangers.

Here are two approaches to resolving the question of adding members:
- Fixed term groups as seen above will solve the problem. There is at least one or two years of settled membership and new members can join at the beginning of the cycle.

- Start groups for new members during the cycle. Some will want to join groups in April or July rather than wait till January. You can start a couple of new groups throughout the year if you have the leaders trained and ready to go.

15.6 EVALUATING GROWTH GROUPS

Should we evaluate?

Evaluating Christian work is different from any other evaluation, because it is assessing God's work. 1 Corinthians 3:1-15 and 4:1-5 teach us how to assess Christian ministry (read them now).

Since God is the source of growth, should we evaluate our groups at all?

Yes—God uses his agents, giving them tasks and entrusting them with the gospel. They are required to be faithful in the task and to the gospel message. It is right to ask whether our work results in the eternal salvation of his people. We should examine our ministry to see whether it is founded and built on Christ, because only such ministry survives the judgment.

There are dangers in human evaluation. We can become proud when, in reality, we are only servants. And as leaders we can suffer false judgements of our ministry based on external appearances, because the true motives of our hearts are concealed—even to ourselves—until Christ is revealed.

What criteria?

From Colossians 1:24-2:5, what criteria would Paul use to assess Growth Groups?
- Have the members been taught and do they understand the word of God—the gospel of Christ?
- Have they responded by putting their faith in Christ?
- Have they rejected human religious systems?
- Do they live in love and unity toward each other?

These are the overriding criteria. If these are not evident, our group needs to return to basics.

Some concrete questions

There are a number of broad areas to evaluate using some specific questions:

Learning the Bible

- What major themes or doctrines have been examined?
- What changes in understanding have members expressed?
- What areas are they still confused about?
- Has new learning taken place, or has it been a case of reinforcing what is familiar?

Prayer

- Is prayer a joy or burden for the group?
- Has the group expanded its prayer concerns?

Personal godliness

- What areas of godly living have members tackled?
- How have relationships between members been shaped by the Bible?

Group life

- Is there more trust between members?
- Who has increased or lowered their level of participation?
- How are members serving each other?

Evangelism

- Is there a concern for the salvation of others?
- Is there a confidence in God's saving power?
- Are members using their gifts and opportunities for the gospel?

Our leadership

This can become too introspective and intimidating, but some questions are worth considering:

- Do I look forward to the group? Why/why not?
- Am I doing everything or are the members sharing in ministry to each other?
- Who do I find difficult in the group? Why? What can be done?
- Do I feel in control?
- What feedback do assistant leaders give?

Growth groups trainee sessions

The course you are about to undertake teaches you how to lead a Growth Group. You will be trained to be 'shepherds' of the flock whom God grants you. You will be responsible for leading these people towards Christlikeness. Treat your training as a Growth Group leader with the importance that it deserves.

This section provides trainee notes for the ten training sessions which make up the course. Before each session, you will need to read the required training topics, as outlined at the end of the previous session. Not all of the training topics will be dealt with in the training sessions. However, it is a good idea to read all of them whilst undertaking this course. The sessions are flexible enough for any further issues raised by these topics to be discussed at appropriate points.

There are different types of exercises used in the training sessions. Some of these are indicated by an icon which explains what kind of activity is being undertaken. The meaning of these icons is explained in detail in the introduction (see pp. 7-8), but it is worth briefly referring to them here. There are three icons:

MIRROR: The mirror exercise gets your training group to reflect upon how it has been operating, in order to learn something about small group dynamics.

 PRACTICE: In a practice exercise, group members practise leading a Bible study based on part of Colossians. Usually, a couple of group members will be asked to observe the rest of the group as one member leads the others in a practice Bible discussion. You will then talk about how the discussion went.

 TOPIC: The topic exercises involve you in a discussion of the training topics set for that session. Sometimes, questions are provided for you to answer; sometimes the discussion will be more free-form.

To summarize, before each session (after Session 1) you need to:
- read the set training topics and be prepared to discuss them
- prepare the Bible study on a section of Colossians.

session 1

1. Participate in an 'ice-breaker' activity organized by your trainer. This activity will be similar to one you might use when you are starting up a Growth Group.

2. Discuss the ice-breaker activity you have just completed.

3. Read through the introduction at the front of this manual. Here you have an opportunity to make sure you understand what training the *Growth Groups* course will provide. Take any notes below.

4. Your trainer will lead you in a study of Colossians 1:1-14. Take any notes below.

5. Provide your trainer with some feedback on the Bible study. Discuss questions such as these:

- Why did some people participate and not others?

- Which questions worked well in discussion? Which didn't? Why was this the case?

- How did group members feel during the discussion?

- What did you observe about other group members?

6. Your trainer will now pray from Colossians 1:1-14. Notice how he uses the passage as a basis for his prayer.

7. Preparation for Session 2:
- Read the following training topics:
    1. *The strategy of Growth Groups*
    2. *Growth Group basics*
    3. *Pitfalls for Growth Groups*
    4. *Preparing a Bible study*
- Use this input to prepare a draft Bible study on Colossians 1:15-23. You might like to photocopy and use the preparation sheet in the appendices for this purpose. This will be discussed and revised in the next training session.

session 2

 1. Your trainer will lead a discussion of the question: What should be the goals of a Growth Group? Take any notes below.

 2. Following is a list of aims that we might have for a small group Bible Study. Mark each aim according to whether you consider it to be:

- essential (√√)
- a good idea (√)
- of limited value (?)
- off the planet (X)

○ *Everyone share their ideas on the passage or topic*
○ *Discuss questions raised by the group*
○ *Pinpoint the main themes of the passage*
○ *Make Bible study fun*
○ *Avoid conflict*
○ *Teach the group how to read the Bible*
○ *Solve all questions and problems raised by the group*
○ *Whet people's appetites for more Bible study*
○ *Teach the main doctrines of the Bible*
○ *Change the way people live*
○ *Memorize Bible passages*
○ *Understand the meaning of details in the passage*

3. Your trainer will lead a discussion of training topic 4: *Preparing a Bible study*. This is your opportunity to discuss and revise your pre-prepared draft Bible study on Colossians 1:15-23. Use the feedback of the group to improve your draft. Take any notes below.

4. Pray as a group about the issues which have been raised.

5. Preparation for Session 3:
- Prepare a Bible study on Colossians 1:24-2:5. One of the trainees will lead this discussion in Session 3, but everyone ought to do the preparation.
- Read the following training topics:
   5. *Leading a Bible study*
   6. *Answers about questions*
   7. *The games people play*

session 3

1. Your trainer will lead a discussion based on training topic 5: *Leading a Bible study*. Answer this question: What are the advantages and disadvantages of the discussion method in Bible study?

2. Your trainer will select a trainee to lead a discussion on Colossians 1:24-2:5 using their prepared study. The discussion will be carefully observed by two appointed groups of observers, who will not participate in the discussion. Each group may consist of only one person, if your training group is small. The observers must not interact with the group, but should remain in the background so as not to inhibit discussion. This is called a *fishbowl* exercise. Other trainees will make up the mock Growth Group.

Observers should use the charts of questions below to assess the discussion. These questions are a summary of training topics 4-7.

Group 1

These observers analyze the **teaching process** during the discussion, using the questions in the table below and overleaf.

QUESTION	YES/NO	COMMENTS
What key truths were communicated? What changes did the group make?		

QUESTION	YES/NO	COMMENTS
Did the launching question work?		
Which observation questions worked?		
Which interpretation questions worked?		
Which summary questions worked?		
Which application questions worked?		
Was the leader a teacher or facilitator?		
Did the leader's control inhibit the discussion?		
Did the group do preparation?		
Did the leader have a flexible plan?		
Did the leader answer questions with questions?		
Did the leader answer his own questions?		
Was each contribution valued and taken on board?		
Did right answers stop discussion?		
Were wrong answers identified?		
Did the group interact with the text of the Bible?		
Did the group ask questions?		
Did the leader preach on hobby horses?		
Was controversy avoided?		
Did the leader pretend to know everything?		

QUESTION	YES/NO	COMMENTS
Did the summary reflect the discussion? Did the summary lead to application and prayer?		

Group 2

These observers analyze the **group participation** during the discussion using these questions.

QUESTION	YES/NO	COMMENTS
What roles did members adopt (e.g. peacemaker, encourager)? Were there sub-groups or cliques? Who are the high/low contributors? What were the reasons for their level of participation? How were the quiet people treated? Was the discussion overly polite, or more open and honest? Which members were focused on tasks? Which members were sensitive to relationships? What was the effect of the physical environment on the discussion?		

3. At the end of the discussion, the observers should give their feedback, with the trainer and all group members joining in the analysis. The feedback should be encouraging and any criticism should be constructive.

Observers might check their interpretations of certain events in the discussion with the group members who were involved. For example, they might enquire whether they rightly understood the reasons for someone not participating. This feedback process sharpens our skills in observing people in discussions and provides insight into what makes discussions succeed or fail.

Take any notes below.

4. Pray as a group about the issues which have been raised.

5. Preparation for Session 4:
- Prepare a study on Colossians 2:6-12.
- Read training topic 8: *Praying in Growth Groups*.
- Prepare a Growth Groups prayer time based on Colossians 2:6-12.

session 4

1. As a group, discuss your preparation of Colossians 2:6-12. Trainees should give examples of:
- teaching goals they have set for the study
- discussion questions

2. Pray together about what you have learnt from Colossians 2:6-12.

3. Use training topic 8: *Praying in Growth Groups* to discuss what was helpful and unhelpful about the prayer time you have just had. Ask yourself questions such as these:
- Did we pray about God's concerns?
- Did we make it easy for everyone to join in?

This is an unusual exercise, since normally we do not need to analyze praying. But it is worth doing for the sake of learning how to lead a group in prayer. Take any notes below.

4. Since this is a shorter session, now is a good time to talk about any issues which have been raised but not addressed so far in the course.

5. Preparation for Session 5:
- Prepare a study on Colossians 2:13-23. One of the trainees will lead this discussion in Session 5, but everyone ought to do the preparation.
- Read training topic 9: *Gospel growth through Growth Groups*.

session 5

 1. Your trainer will select a trainee to lead a discussion on Colossians 2:13-23 using their prepared study. Again, the discussion will be carefully observed by two appointed groups of observers, who will not participate in the discussion. Other trainees will make up the mock Growth Group.

Observers use the charts of questions below to assess the discussion.

Group 1

These observers analyze the **teaching process** during the discussion, using the questions in the table below.

QUESTION	YES/NO	COMMENTS
What key truths were communicated?		
What changes did the group make?		
Did the launching question work?		
Which observation questions worked?		
Which interpretation questions worked?		
Which summary questions worked?		
Which application questions worked?		
Was the leader a teacher or facilitator?		
Did the leader's control inhibit the discussion?		
Did the group do preparation?		

QUESTION	YES/NO	COMMENTS
Did the leader have a flexible plan?		
Did the leader answer questions with questions?		
Did the leader answer their own questions?		
Was each contribution valued and taken on board?		
Did right answers stop discussion?		
Were wrong answers identified?		
Did the group interact with the text of the Bible?		
Did the group ask questions?		
Did the leader preach on hobby horses?		
Was controversy avoided?		
Did the leader pretend to know everything?		
Did the summary reflect the discussion?		
Did the summary lead to application and prayer?		

Group 2

These observers analyze the **group participation** during the discussion using these questions.

QUESTION	YES/NO	COMMENTS
What roles did members adopt (e.g. peacemaker, encourager)?		
Were there sub-groups or cliques?		
Who are the high/low contributors?		
What were the reasons for their level of participation?		
How were the quiet people treated?		
Was the discussion overly polite, or more open and honest?		
Which members were focused on tasks?		
Which members were sensitive to relationships?		
What was the effect of the physical environment on the discussion?		

2. At the end of the discussion, the observers should give their feedback, with the trainer and all group members joining in the analysis. The feedback should be encouraging and any criticism should be constructive. As before, observers should discuss their interpretations of the group's words and actions with the members involved, to hone their observational skills. Take any notes below.

3. Your trainer will lead you in a discussion of training topic 9: *Gospel growth through Growth Groups*. Discuss the following issues:
   i. Why should Growth Groups be active in evangelism?

   ii. Why do Growth Groups find evangelism difficult?

   iii. What can we do in Growth Groups to engage in evangelism?

4. Pray together about evangelism.

5. Preparation for Session 6:
 • Prepare a Bible study on Colossians 3:1-11.
 • Read training topic 10: *Leading for growth*.

session 6

 1. As a group, discuss your preparation of Colossians 3:1-11. Trainees should give examples of:
- teaching goals they have set for the study
- discussion questions

2. Pray as a group about the issues which have been raised.

 3. Your trainer will lead you in a discussion of some of the issues raised in training topic 10: *Leading for growth*. In the discussion, endeavour to answer some of the questions below.

   i. What are the positive and negative effects of running Growth Groups without a designated leader?

   ii. What biblical reasons exist for having designated leaders?

   iii. What makes a Christian leader (see Col 1:24-2:5; 1 Pet 5:1-4)?

iv. What symptoms suggest that a leader is being self-serving in a group?

v. Is there an optimum leadership style for Growth Groups? Give reasons for your answer.

vi. What is the role of a co-leader when another leader is running the discussion?

vii. What will it mean to properly use your personality in leadership?

4. Preparation for Session 7:
- Prepare a Bible study on Colossians 3:12-17. One of the trainees will lead this discussion in Session 7, but everyone ought to do the preparation.
- Read training topic 11: *Growing the individuals.*

session 7

 1. Your trainer will select a trainee to lead a study on Colossians 3:12-17 using their prepared study. Again, the discussion will be carefully observed by two appointed groups of observers, who will not participate in the discussion. Other trainees will make up the mock Growth Group.

Observers use the charts of questions below to assess the discussion.

Group 1

These observers analyze the **teaching process** during the discussion, using the questions in the table below.

QUESTION	YES/NO	COMMENTS
What key truths were communicated?		
What changes did the group make?		
Did the launching question work?		
Which observation questions worked?		
Which interpretation questions worked?		
Which summary questions worked?		
Which application questions worked?		
Was the leader a teacher or facilitator?		
Did the leader's control inhibit the discussion?		
Did the group do preparation?		
Did the leader have a flexible plan?		

QUESTION	YES/NO	COMMENTS
Did the leader answer questions with questions?		
Did the leader answer their own questions?		
Was each contribution valued and taken on board?		
Did right answers stop discussion?		
Were wrong answers identified?		
Did the group interact with the text of the Bible?		
Did the group ask questions?		
Did the leader preach on hobby horses?		
Was controversy avoided?		
Did the leader pretend to know everything?		
Did the summary reflect the discussion?		
Did the summary lead to application and prayer?		

Group 2

These observers analyze the **group participation** during the discussion using these questions.

QUESTION	YES/NO	COMMENTS
What roles did members adopt (e.g. peacemaker, encourager)?		
Were there sub-groups or cliques?		
Who are the high/low contributors?		
What were the reasons for their level of participation?		
How were the quiet people treated?		
Was the discussion overly polite, or more open and honest?		
Which members were focused on tasks?		
Which members were sensitive to relationships?		
What was the effect of the physical environment on the discussion?		

2. At the end of the discussion, the observers give their feedback, the trainer and all group members entering into the analysis. As usual, feedback should be encouraging and any criticism should be constructive. Take any notes below.

3. Your trainer will lead a discussion based on training topic 11: *Growing the individuals*. During the discussion, answer the following questions.

  i. Which has more influence on a Growth Group: God's agenda or the People's agenda?

  ii. Why are we often tempted to serve the group structures rather than the individuals in the group?

  iii. How should we deal with 'problem people' in our groups?

  iv. How is training future leaders an important part of growing your individual group members?

4. Pray together about what you have learnt from the Bible study of Colossians 3:12-17.

5. Preparation for Session 8:
- Prepare a Bible study on Colossians 3:18-4:1.
- Read training topic 12: *The healthy Growth Group*.

session 8

 1. As a group, discuss your preparation of Colossians 3:18-4:1. Trainees should give examples of:
- teaching goals they have set for the study
- discussion questions

 2. Your trainer will lead a discussion of training topic 12: *The healthy Growth Group*. Many of the relevant issues have already been raised in other exercises throughout the course. Use this opportunity to clarify your aims and goals for Growth Groups. In the discussion, answer the following questions:

    i. From Colossians 3:1-17, what should characterize the relationships within a Growth Group?

    ii. What are healthy ground rules for group behaviour and interaction?

iii. How can we encourage members to use their gifts to benefit the group?

3. Use training topic 12 to make a diagnosis of the health of our training group. Follow the three stages as set out. Take any notes below.
- Make accurate observations: using the diagnostic tool at 12.1

- Determine the cause(s) of ill-health: using the possible causes listed at 12.2

- Apply the remedy: decide on specific action to be taken

4. Pray for the skills we need in understanding people.

5. Preparation for Session 9:
- Prepare a Bible study on Colossians 4:2-18. One of the trainees will lead this discussion in Session 10, but everyone ought to do the preparation.
- Read training topic 13: *Starting a Growth Group*.

session 9

 1. Your trainer will select a trainee to lead a discussion on Colossians 4:2-18 using their prepared study. Again, the discussion will be carefully observed by two appointed groups of observers, who will not participate in the discussion. Other trainees will make up the mock Growth Group.

Observers use the charts of questions below to assess the discussion.

Group 1

These observers analyze the **teaching process** during the discussion, using the questions in the table below.

QUESTION	YES/NO	COMMENTS
What key truths were communicated?		
What changes did the group make?		
Did the launching question work?		
Which observation questions worked?		
Which interpretation questions worked?		
Which summary questions worked?		
Which application questions worked?		
Was the leader a teacher or facilitator?		
Did the leader's control inhibit the discussion?		
Did the group do preparation?		

QUESTION	YES/NO	COMMENTS
Did the leader have a flexible plan?		
Did the leader answer questions with questions?		
Did the leader answer their own questions?		
Was each contribution valued and taken on board?		
Did right answers stop discussion?		
Were wrong answers identified?		
Did the group interact with the text of the Bible?		
Did the group ask questions?		
Did the leader preach on hobby horses?		
Was controversy avoided?		
Did the leader pretend to know everything?		
Did the summary reflect the discussion?		
Did the summary lead to application and prayer?		

Group 2

These observers analyze the **group participation** during the discussion using these questions.

QUESTION	YES/NO	COMMENTS
What roles did members adopt (e.g. peacemaker, encourager)?		
Were there sub-groups or cliques?		
Who are the high/low contributors?		
What were the reasons for their level of participation?		
How were the quiet people treated?		
Was the discussion overly polite, or more open and honest?		
Which members were focused on tasks?		
Which members were sensitive to relationships?		
What was the effect of the physical environment on the discussion?		

 2. At the end of the discussion, the observers should give their feedback, with the trainer and all group members joining in the analysis. The feedback should be encouraging and any criticism should be constructive. As before, observers should discuss their interpretations of the group's words and actions with the members involved, to hone their observational skills. Take any notes below.

3. Your trainer will lead a discussion of training topic 13: *Starting a Growth Group*. Answer these questions during the discussion.

i. How does it affect a new group when the group's purpose and agenda are not set out clearly?

ii. What reasons might people have for joining a Growth Group?

iii. What commitments should be spelt out as we start a group?

iv. What stage in the life of a group has this training group reached?

4. Pray as a group, thanking God for the different gifts of the people in your training group.

5. Preparation for Session 10:
- Read the following training topics:

    14. *Selecting, training and shepherding leaders*

    15. *Developing the Growth Group program*
- Review what has been achieved through the training course using these questions:

    —Have the training goals and objectives in the introduction been achieved?

    —How have you personally benefitted?

    —How can you use this training?

session 10

1. Pray about your current and future ministries and how you will use this training.

 2. Your trainer will lead a discussion of training topics 14: *Selecting, training and shepherding leaders* and 15: *Developing the Growth Group program*. In the discussion, answer the following questions and take any notes below.

    i. Are there any other benefits of Growth Groups not discussed in training topic 15?

    ii. What are the dangers in setting up Growth Groups?

iii. What factors need to be considered when deciding how to end a Growth Group?

iv. What leadership training should be developed in your church or ministry?

 3. Your trainer will guide you through the process of evaluating a Growth Group, using this training group as a case study. In the process of evaluation, do the following exercises.
Read 1 Corinthians 3:5-15, 4:1-5:

i. Since God is the source of growth, should we evaluate our groups at all?

ii. What are the dangers of human evaluation?

iii. How does God evaluate his workers?

Read Colossians 1:24-2:5:

    i. What criteria would Paul use to assess the Growth Group at Colossae?

    ii. Has this training group been taught and understood the word of God—the gospel of Christ?

    iii. Have its members responded by faith in Christ, rejection of false human religion, love and unity toward each other?

Answer these questions yourself, in relation to this training group:

- Did I look forward to the group? Why/why not?

- Was the trainer doing everything or were the members sharing in ministry to each other?

- Who did I find difficult in the group? Why? What could have been done?

- Did I feel in control?

- What feedback did the group give to the trainer?

4. This is one small group which definitely has an expiry date! You have reached the end of the *Growth Groups* training course. It's time now to review the benefits of the course. Your trainer will lead you in a discussion of the review questions from your preparation (see the end of Session 9).

appendix i

Other useful resources

SPECIALIST RESOURCES FROM MATTHIAS MEDIA

Matthias Media (Sydney, Australia) publishes resources for growing Christians. Their aim is very similar to that of Growth Groups: to 'grow' more Christians through evangelism, and to grow Christians in maturity as they submit to Christ. Following is a list of books, courses and other resources which Matthias Media produces.[1] Many of these are designed especially for use in small groups.

Interactive Bible Studies

Interactive Bible Studies are a bit like a guided tour of a city. They take you on a journey through a book or section of the Bible, pointing out things along the way, filling in some background details and suggesting avenues for further exploration. But they also provide plenty of opportunity for doing sightseeing of your own—wandering off, having a good look around and forming your own conclusions.

The Interactive Bible Studies series is growing all the time, with many

---

1   For more information about Matthias Media, see page 180.

new titles published each year. Here is a list of the titles available at the time this book was published:

Beyond Eden (Genesis 1-11)

Out of Darkness (Exodus 1-18)

The Shadow of Glory (Exodus 19-40)

The One and Only (Deuteronomy)

The Good, The Bad and The Ugly (Judges)

Famine and Fortune (Ruth)

Renovator's Dream (Nehemiah)

The Eye of the Storm (Job)

The Search for Meaning (Ecclesiastes)

Two Cities (Isaiah)

Kingdom of Dreams (Daniel)

Burning Desire (Obadiah and Malachi)

Warning Signs (Jonah)

On That Day (Zechariah)

Full of Promise (The big picture of the O.T.)

The Good Living Guide (Matthew 5:1-12)

News of the Hour (Mark)

Proclaiming the Risen Lord (Luke 24-Acts 2)

Mission Unstoppable (Acts)

The Free Gift of Life (Romans 1-5)

The Free Gift of Sonship (Romans 6-11)

Free for All (Galatians)

Walk this Way (Ephesians)

Partners for Life (Philippians)

The Complete Christian (Colossians)

To the Householder (1 Timothy)

Run the Race (2 Timothy)

The Path to Godliness (Titus)

From Shadow to Reality (Hebrews)

The Implanted Word (James)

Homeward Bound (1 Peter)

All You Need to Know (2 Peter)

The Vision Statement (Revelation)

A series of Topical Bible Studies, which examines important themes in light of the Scriptures, is also under way. Four titles are currently available:

Bold I Approach (Prayer)

Cash Values (Money)

The Blueprint (Doctrine)

Woman of God (The Bible on Women)

New titles in the Interactive Bible Studies series are regularly being added to this list. Call us or visit our website for the latest information. See page 180 for contact details.

Pathway Bible Guides

This series of study guides provides studies which are a little shorter and simpler than the Interactive Bible Studies series. They are ideal for groups with a bit less time or more limited experience in Bible study. At the time of publishing, the following books are available in the PBG series:

Beginning with God (Genesis 1-12)
Getting to Know God (Exodus 1-20)
The Art of Living (Proverbs)
Seeing Things God's Way (Daniel)
Fear and Freedom (Matthew 8-12)
Following Jesus (Luke 9-12)
Peace with God (Romans)
Church Matters (1 Corinthians 1-7)
Standing Firm (1 Thessalonians)

Insight Bible Studies

The Insight Bible Studies are studies which utilize video input to help groups explore an important topic of the Christian life. There are currently two in the series:

Where to, Lord? (Guidance)
From Sinner to Saint (Holiness)

Studies for new Christians

Back to Basics: 7 basic Bible studies on Christian living.

Resources for evangelism

Two Ways To Live: The choice we all face: a popular giveaway gospel presentation.
Two Ways To Live CD-ROM: a multimedia gospel presentation.
Two Ways To Live Bible study: a one-hour Bible study explaining the gospel.
Tough Questions: 5 short studies from the Gospel of Mark, for use with enquirers.
Investigating Christianity: 4 short studies on the big questions about life, for use with enquirers.
Simply Christianity: A 5-week introduction to Jesus for non-Christians through Luke's Gospel.

Training Courses

Six Steps to Encouragement: How words change lives: a course in the how and why of personal encouragement.
Six Steps to Talking about Jesus: a course designed to help all Christians get started in sharing their faith.
Six Steps to Reading Your Bible: a course designed to help all Christians get into regular and enjoyable Bible reading.

Two Ways To Live: Know and share the gospel: a friendly, easy-to-use course for training your group in knowing and sharing the gospel.

The Bible Overview: take a group through the 'big picture' of the Bible.

So Many Questions: how to answer common questions about Christianity.

AIDS TO BIBLE STUDY

Commentaries: there are numerous commentaries on books of the Bible. They can be very useful when preparing a Bible study. Use them selectively, always reading the passage for yourself before turning to the commentary. Some good commentary series include the 'Tyndale' commentaries and the 'New International Commentary' series. Commentary surveys are also available, such as DA Carson's *New Testament Commentary Survey*.

New Bible Dictionary and *New Bible Commentary*: two very handy volumes for every Growth Group leader.

Postcard from Palestine by Andrew Reid (Matthias Media): a hands-on guide to interpreting the Bible.

Gospel and Kingdom by Graeme Goldsworthy (Paternoster Press): an excellent and easy-to-read introduction to biblical theology.

BOOKS ABOUT SMALL GROUP LEADERSHIP

Getting Together by Em Griffin (IVP, 1982)

How to Lead Small Group Bible Studies (NavPress, 1982)

Leading Better Bible Studies by Rod and Karen Morris (Aquila, 1997)

OTHER RESOURCES

Know and Tell the Gospel by John Chapman (Matthias Media): entertaining and straightforward advice on sharing the gospel with others.

Operation World edited by Patrick Johnstone (WEC publishing): a directory of the state of the church around the world. Handy for group prayer.

The Briefing is a magazine published 12 times per year by Matthias Media and regularly contains articles, book reviews and resources relevant to Growth Group leaders. A CD-ROM archive of over 2000 articles is also available.

appendix ii

Using pre-packaged Bible studies

There are many pre-packaged Bible studies on the market, some designed for personal study and others for small group discussion.[1] *There are many benefits to using well designed studies* in attractive formats which are committed to sound biblical interpretation. In practice, a combination of Bible studies you have prepared yourself and pre-packaged ones provides a healthy variety of input for your group.

TIPS FOR USING PRE-PACKAGED BIBLE STUDIES

Leading a Growth Group using published Bible studies would appear to reduce the preparation time for the leader, but it presents some potential pitfalls. In some ways, it requires more preparation to make the teaching effective.

- Study the passage independently of the study notes.[2] This will give you a clear grasp of the central and supporting truths, and major applications

---

1 See appendix I.
2 Use the steps in training topic 4: *Preparing a Bible study.*

and possible teaching goals. It means you are not entirely depending on another author's interpretation and emphases. It will also help you to understand the author's design and intention for the study.

- Prepare discussion questions beyond the questions in the published study.[3] Sometimes the published questions are designed more for private study and need supplementing if you are going to create discussion. Your own questions also achieve your teaching goals and can stretch the group further than does their private preparation.

LEARNING TO WRITE YOUR OWN BIBLE STUDIES

This course on Growth Groups offers training in preparing your own Bible studies. While recognizing the value of pre-packaged material, there are benefits in knowing how to prepare from scratch.

- You learn the principles of Bible reading.
- You tend to be more enthusiastic about material you have prepared.
- You can tailor a study on any passage for particular groups to achieve particular goals.
- It is good to demonstrate to the group not to be dependent on study guides.
- You will make better use of prepared studies.
- You will be more discerning in evaluating prepared studies.

---

3   Use training topic 5: *Leading a Bible study.*

appendix (iii)

Preparation sheet

STEP 1: Understanding the passage

Overview of the book

Overview of the passage

Question bombardment

Background

Flow of the passage

The passage in context

Central truth and supporting truths

STEP 2: Applying the passage

The person

The group

The church

The world

STEP 3: Working out teaching goals

Central truth

Supporting truths

Applications

STEP 4: Packaging the study

Observation questions

Interpretation questions

Correlation questions

Summary questions

Application questions

Launching question

Sample Bible study preparation:
COLOSSIANS 1:1-14

STEP 1: Understanding the passage

Overview of the book

main themes:
- —who Christ is and how he saves
- —living with Christ as Lord

repeated words and phrases:
- *fullness, complete, thankful, understanding, knowledge, wisdom, grow, power*

structure:
- —*teaching about Christ and salvation in Christ (ch. 1-2)*
- —*application of this teaching (ch. 3-4)*

the author:
- —*Paul, an apostle in prison (4:3, 10)*
- —*has not met the Colossians (2:1)*
- —*his mission to proclaim Christ to the Gentile world (1:24-27)*
- —*he is passionate for Christ and a servant of his church*
- —*he is sending Tychicus and Onesimus to Colossae (4:7-9)*

the recipients:

    —*Christians at Colossae (1:2)*

    —*also to be read to the Laodiceans (4:16)*

    —*Epaphras from Colossae told them the gospel (1:7)*

    —*they are exposed to other religious philosophies*

author's purpose:

    —*they have received Christ Jesus as Lord and now must continue to live in him and not be captivated by other philosophies (2:6-8)*

    —*they need no more than Christ who is the fullness of God and the ruler of all (2:9-10)*

    —*Christ, through his death and resurrection, is all they need for salvation and overcoming their corrupt nature (2:11-3:5)*

Overview of the passage (1:1-14)

stands out:

    —*Father, Son and Spirit were active in the Colossians*

    —*profound changes have occurred in the Colossians*

    —*thankfulness dominates Paul's attitude*

difficulties:

    —*why do faith and love spring from hope? (vv. 4-5)*

    —*what is the kingdom of light? (v. 12)*

repeated key words:

    —*thank, faith, love, hope, truth, gospel, grow, knowledge, kingdom, bearing fruit*

repeated ideas:

    —*hearing the gospel or truth, prayer, thankfulness, faith*

commands:

    —*live worthy of the Lord and please him (v. 10)*

the author:

    —*Paul an apostle along with Timothy (v. 1)*

    —*Epaphras works on behalf of Paul (v. 7)*

    —*Paul takes spiritual responsibility for the Colossians and prays for them*

the recipients:

    —*their faith and love is renowned (v. 4)*

main ideas:

   —*God is saving and changing people*
   —*God works through the gospel and his servants*

Question bombardment

unfamiliar words:

   —*spiritual wisdom? (v. 9)*
   —*redemption? (v. 14)*
   —*dominion of darkness? (v. 13)*

Background

customs:

   —*redemption in Old Testament*

contribution to the book:

   —*elaborates the complete work done by God through the gospel of his Son*
   —*the Colossians are the genuine fruit of the true gospel, over against the false teachers and their philosophies*

immediate context:

   —*Paul goes on to explain the lordship of Christ over all and his reconciling work on the cross (1:15-23)*

Flow of the passage

   —*introduction and greeting (vv. 1-2)*
   —*Paul's thankfulness (vv. 3-5) for their faith, hope and love*
   —*The fruit of the gospel (vv. 6-8) at Colossae and worldwide*
   —*Paul's prayer (vv. 9-14) for knowledge of God's will resulting in conduct pleasing the Lord bearing the fruit of good works growing in the knowledge of God enabled by God's strengthening power giving thanks for his saving work*

The passage in context

biblical themes:

   —*the sovereignty of God in salvation*
   —*God's use of human agents*

stage of God's saving work:

   —*after the death and resurrection of Christ and before the final judgment, when Christ is building his church, through the ministry of the gospel*

Jesus' identity and purpose:

    —the Son of the Father

    —he rescues, redeems and forgives

Central truths and supporting truths

central truth:

    —God saves and transforms people

    —God works through:

- *prayer: God himself is the agent of change (vv. 3, 9)*
- *proclamation: of the gospel of Christ (vv. 5, 7)*
- *people: God uses his servants to teach Christ (vv. 1, 7)*

STEP 2: Applying the passage

The person

    —assurance of God's saving work in us

    —a call to prayer and gospelling

    —cultivating thankfulness

The group

    —the agenda for Christian groups: salvation and transformation through prayer and the gospel of truth

The church

    —discerning a true work of God over against a false ministry

The world

    —the hopelessness of changing society without changing people

STEP 3: Working out teaching goals

Central truth

    —God saves and transforms people

Supporting truths

    —God works through:

- *prayer: God himself is the agent of change (vv. 3, 9)*

- *proclamation: of the gospel of Christ (vv. 5, 7)*
- *people: God uses his servants to teach Christ (vv. 1, 7)*

Applications
the agenda for Christian groups:

—*salvation and transformation through prayer and the gospel of truth*

STEP 4: Packaging the study
Observation questions
What has God already done for the Colossians?
What is God's ongoing work for them?
How does God accomplish his work?

Interpretation questions
What is the gospel?
What is the prerequisite for living a life worthy of the Lord? Why is this ? (vv. 9, 10)
What was the effect of God's power on the Colossians? (vv. 11-14)

Correlation questions
What is the gospel according to 1:21-23?
Where else in Colossians is the idea of filling or fullness? (v. 9)

Summary questions
What is God's purpose in the world?
How does God achieve this purpose?

Application question
From this passage, what implications can we draw concerning the goals and methods of gospel ministry?

Launching question
Imagine you are a reporter for the Colossae Herald and you are interviewing this group Paul is writing to. You want to know what exactly has happened to them. What would they say?

matthiasmedia

Matthias Media is a ministry team of like-minded, evangelical Christians working together to achieve a particular goal, as summarized in our mission statement:

To serve our Lord Jesus Christ, and the growth of his gospel in the world, by producing and delivering high quality, Bible-based resources.

It was in 1988 that we first started pursuing this mission together, and in God's kindness we now have more than 250 different ministry resources being distributed all over the world. These resources range from Bible studies and books, through to training courses and audio sermons.

To find out more about our large range of very useful products, and to access samples and free downloads, visit our website:

www.matthiasmedia.com.au

How to buy our resources
1. Direct from us over the internet:
   – in the US: www.matthiasmedia.com
   – in Australia and the rest of the world: www.matthiasmedia.com.au

2. Direct from us by phone:
   – in the US: 1 866 407 4530
   – in Australia: 1800 814 360 (Sydney: 9663 1478)
   – international: +61-2-9663-1478

3. Through a range of outlets in various parts of the world. Visit **www.matthiasmedia.com.au/international.php** for details about recommended retailers in your part of the world, including www.thegoodbook.co.uk in the United Kingdom.

4. Trade enquiries can be addressed to:
   – in the US: sales@matthiasmedia.com
   – in the UK: sales@ivpbooks.com
   – in Australia and the rest of the world: sales@matthiasmedia.com.au